MW01030732

How to Start a Private Investigation Business:
A Proven Blueprint for Success
By Edward Panico

Disclaimers & Copyright

the purchaser or the reader of these materials. Any perceived slight of any individual or organization is purely unintentional.

Nothing in this book constitutes an endorsement or reflects the official position of the U.S. Department of State, U.S. Department of Defense, U.S. Intelligence Community or any other government entity. The opinions and positions are the author's alone. Information contained in this book should not be construed as legal, financial or accounting advice nor is it intended to be a substitute for legal counsel on any subject matter.

Resources marked with an (*) are affiliate products, meaning the author receives a referral fee on any purchase at no extra expense to the purchaser. All products recommended have been tested by the author. Reader or purchasers are advised to do their own research before making any purchase online. No guarantees of earnings or other results – of any kind – nor any liability is assumed for the publisher or author. The reader is entirely responsible for his or her own actions.

Printed in the United States of America

Lynx Security Solutions LLC

96 Linwood Plaza #455

Fort Lee, NJ 07024

Dedication

To my daughter Annabelle who I love so much. Everything I have done, that I am doing, and that I am going to do, is for you.

Preface

"Believe you can and you're halfway there."
-Theodore Roosevelt

Congratulations on taking a step towards the field of private investigation as a business owner. Small business owners are the lifeblood of the American economy. Your appetite for risk has the potential for you to create jobs and solve client's problems, while making you a healthy income. Business is one of the fastest ways to generate wealth, far exceeding anything a standard job could do in this field while simultaneously helping people along the way. At my organization Lynx Security Group (Lynx), and its sister companies, we have solved problems for clients ranging from uncovering infidelity to enforcing contracts and disproving cyberbullying. As long as it is legal and ethical, you'll find the potential to help those in need never ending in this field.

Every year, thousands of people come of legal licensing age for entry into this private sector field. Those that don't come from a government background wonder if they can compete with those that have. One of the most common misconceptions of this field is that you need experience either as a career homicide detective, or a former Special Agent with the Federal

Bureau of Investigation who worked transnational organized crime cases to succeed. Nothing is further from the truth. Some of the best field investigators who work for Lynx never served a day in this capacity. Instead, their attention to detail, ingenuity, and dedication to uncovering the facts made them stand out above their peers.

Besides those who come straight from the private sector, thousands of people leave law enforcement, the Intelligence Community, and the military every year. They wonder if they can leverage skills gained in these entities and put them to use in the private sector. The answer, of course, is yes. As someone who has straddled both the private sector and public sector over the last several years, the biggest thing you will have to overcome is failing to try because the safety net might not be there to catch you. It might be daunting at first, but it is not insurmountable.

This book shows you *a* way, not *the* way, of starting your private investigation business. I hope you can avoid the failures I made starting out and build on the foundations of success I have had. I am not too concerned with competition, which is something often shunned today in the "everyone gets a trophy" environment. Competition is healthy for an economy because it forces you to continue improving and innovating to stand out from your peers. There are enough cases out there and money to go around for all. The road is long, but the success and recognition that lies on the horizon makes all the difference.

Table of Contents

Chapter 1
Foundations

"Every man at the bottom of his heart believes that he is a born detective."
- John Buchan

Private Investigation Defined

Before you consider starting your private investigation company, we need to define what a private investigator is and if this field is for you. What is a private investigator? (a.k.a. private eye, private dick, private detective, professional investigator, etc.) The term conjures up images of film noir like The Maltese Falcon, the modern reboot of Magnum P.I., or even the former superhero Jessica Jones. All 50 states and Washington D.C. have their own definition of the profession such as Maryland Code Section 13-101 or California Business and Professions Code Chapter 11.3., Section 7512.

You will also find different definitions and terms internationally, such as those found in the United Kingdom's Private Security Industry Act of 2001 schedule 2, paragraph 4(1). The closest thing to a universal board certification the field has is the private organization ASIS International (formerly known as the American Society of Industrial Security). With so many variations in this profession and even its name, and so many people getting their information sources from the media, it's no wonder clients have no idea what we do.

So, what is a private investigator? If you are looking for a formal definition, the Virginia Department of Criminal Justice Services has a pretty solid one: "A private investigator means any individual who engages in the business of, or accepts employment to make, investigations to obtain information on crimes or civil wrongs; the location, disposition, or recovery of stolen property; the cause of accidents, fires, damages, or injuries to persons or to property; or evidence to be used before any court, board, officer, or investigative committee." If you want something shorter, an independent fact finder who works in the private sector for compensation will do.

Harry Sonneborn famously stated, "We [McDonald's] are not technically in the food business. We are in the real estate business." I have news for you. Investigators are not in the investigations business. They are actually in the information and fact-finding business. That is what people are after, and that is what you actually are providing regardless of the case you take on. All your actions are a systematic process towards the gathering of factual information for your client. If you remember this, it will serve you well as you proceed in the business.

Private Investigator Traits

What are some traits that make a good private investigator stand out? Many come to mind, but some are attention to detail, persistence, trustworthiness, passion, people skills, and innovation. Let's explore these traits briefly.

Those with attention to detail routinely latch onto the one fact that blows the case wide open, such as when one of my investigators noticed an anomaly with phone calls on every Thursday from the subject of the investigation's phone record to the mistress we identified.

Persistence comes into play with cases that go the distance. Many private investigation cases, specifically in the insurance realm, are closed the same day, but in the domestic space they can last a long time. We assisted with litigation on a case for a year and a half before we knew it. Another client came to us after she had already cycled through several attorneys and private investigation companies. They had been working her case for approximately two years. Another had been in and out of court for seven years!

Trustworthiness. Nothing will get you dropped quicker in this profession than being untrustworthy. Lynx does not take on cases unless they are legal and ethical. However, for every company like Lynx, there are 100 no-questions-asked private investigation companies. More on this and the danger it presents later.

Those without a passion for uncovering facts won't last long in this field. Some of the investigator's foundational skillset like physical surveillance, report writing, investigative interviewing, evidence collection, and database research can be quite boring. Once you realize it is not all high-speed chases, martial arts and shootouts, those without passion won't make it far.

The ability to relate to people and to talk to them is paramount in furthering your investigation. You do not have to be an extrovert, but you need to hold a conversation and develop rapport with those you are interviewing. You will quickly realize you have to talk to a variety of people from a variety of backgrounds to get the information you need. You also need to show empathy to clients who may be at a very low point in their life (cheating spouse, child custody dispute, or business on the ropes) as much as you show it to the overworked claims manager or public defender.

Finally, innovation. If you can't innovate, you will get left behind in this field. Technology gets better every day, and it's important to think outside the box when it comes to tools at your disposal. Lynx has utilized drones for difficult physical surveillance situations and complex evidence collection techniques such as forensic mitochondrial DNA analysis by using one of our independent laboratory partners.

The investigators I have worked with who have exhibited these qualities are the ones that go the distance in this field. Others will eventually exhaust themselves and transition to another profession and wonder why they never gained traction.

Private Sector vs. Public Sector Investigation

There are two distinct categories of investigation: those in the private sector and those in the public sector. Private sector investigations are usually found in private investigation firms or as in-house corporate investigators for the countless companies incorporated worldwide. The public sector ones are those primarily from law enforcement whether it be at the local, state, or federal level. There are numerous agencies at these levels across the U.S. and the world. These agencies are normally charged with criminal investigation duties and fall short of the assortment of sub-categories a private investigator may investigate. Some differences include types of investigation, an investigative mandate, and investigative techniques authorized.

In the public sector, the scope of an investigation is normally limited to involving a criminal or intelligence nexus. The local police won't help you investigate if your boyfriend is cheating on you. Nor will they run credit checks and financial information checks for your company if you plan a merger with another company. Since private investigators really are not restricted to what they can investigate as long as its legal and ethical, virtually anything can fit the bill. Thus, the investigation can be something as benign as a premise's liability claim to a cheating spouse to something more complex like a criminal investigation involving a homicide.

If you work in a public sector investigation organization, and you are assigned a case, you can't just say, "I won't work on this." You have a mandate to investigate and provide for the public's good. However, in private investigation, you may take on or turn down as many cases as you want. If a potential client seems difficult to work with, you can turn them down. You are only limited by time and the amount of manpower you have accessible.

Public sector investigation organizations normally have a broad range of authorized investigative techniques, resources, and a large budget to support them. Public investigators have a litany of special databases just for them such as the National

Crime Information Center that make running a criminal records check a breeze. Private investigators can utilize several of the public investigator's databases. Public investigators usually have their own crime lab where they can submit evidence, while a private investigator might have to hire a private lab to run results for them. Since public investigators run off tax payer dollars, they are only limited by their organization's budget. The private investigator is limited by their client's budget which might be low or have no ceiling, especially when it involves children.

Those coming from the public sector into the private sector sometimes experience a shock. Some are used to having cases being brought to them, but quickly realize if you don't take a proactive approach, you might not have any clients and start going hungry. Others who nonchalantly threw around government resources because bureaucratic top cover protected them are quick to realize that when it's your business you are liable for any mistakes made. In this sense, those who never worked in the public sector have the advantage because they have had to hustle since day one. The overall comparison is like apples and oranges. One is not better than the other and they both serve their purposes in a free society.

Types of Private Investigation

If you thought the range of private investigator characters in literature, movies, television, and the real world weren't enough, consider that we have not even touched on what types of investigations those investigators engage in. Entire books are dedicated to the specialist fields within the private investigation realm. Most go by several names and the techniques used in them cross pollinate to other investigative fields. Here are some of the broad categories in alphabetical order:

- Accident Investigation

- Asset Investigation

- Corporate Investigation

- Criminal Investigation

- Cyber Investigation

- Domestic Investigation

- Fraud Investigation

- Insurance Investigation

- Missing Persons Investigation

- Technical Investigation

  These will be explored in the next chapter.

Chapter 2
Types of Investigation

"Pleasure in the job puts perfection in the work."
-Aristotle

Accident Investigation

Accident investigations are the systematic review of an accident to determine the root cause or, in the private investigation realm, who was at fault. Accident investigations normally come from an attorney or insurance company looking at liability circumstances that minimize (or even eliminate) a monetary payout. Therefore, accident investigations are commonly placed under the umbrella of insurance investigations. Lynx was asked to assist another private investigation company to locate a Sport Utility Vehicle (SUV) that cut an 18-wheeler off and caused it to flip on the highway. The SUV sped off, the truck and other vehicles were damaged, and people injured. Naturally, the insurance company wanted to protect their interest by proving the SUV driver was at fault and not the truck driver. Lynx assisted with photograph enhancement so the investigation company could read the license plate and find the vehicle.

At the time of writing, the case was ongoing.

Often clients will employ private investigators because they feel the police have not investigated the accident as deeply as they would like. In many police departments, unless someone is killed or seriously injured there is no in-depth accident investigation. In fact, if there are no injuries and the vehicular damage is minimal, there may not even be a police investigation. This leaves the involved party looking for answers, which is where a private investigator comes in.

Many state troopers end up with a background in accident investigation due to their time on the highways responding to crashes. Subsequently, they move into this field. But accident investigation is not just limited to collisions and to those who used to be state law enforcement. The category is broader and includes boating accidents, snowmobile accidents, plane crashes, drownings, and building collapse. This enables you to carve out a niche and make a tidy profit, especially if you are labeled an expert witness. There are a few training schools and courses available to the private sector such as Texas A&M's Extension Service accident investigation suite which primarily focuses on vehicle accidents. One can gain skills in scene reconstruction, analysis of tire skids, steering systems, and vehicle dynamics. Study of topics such as geometry and physics also prepare an aspiring investigator in this field.

Asset Investigation

Asset investigation is another broad category that commonly falls under domestic investigation. Asset investigation is the methodical search (and sometimes retrieval) of tangible and intangible assets through public records searches and other investigative means. They are common in divorce proceedings where the hiring attorney or client wants a complete picture of assets available, including any hidden ones, in order for the court to allocate and distribute them appropriately under a process known as equitable distribution. Private investigators rarely have complete access or authority to access bank accounts. They need to work in tandem with an attorney to subpoena the bank or investment firm once they discover they exist. Public record searches, physical surveillance, computer forensics, and elicitation during interviews are some skills that can help identify hidden assets.

Some private investigation companies who specialize in asset identification and retrieval base fees on taking a portion of the assets recovered—a typical fee is 33 percent. It would surprise you how many larger companies take up this offer because 67 percent recovered is better than zero percent. You would be more surprised to learn this also applies to investigation companies that help uncover hidden assets for people involved in child support payment disputes. These emotionally charged events make people more than willing to make similar payment arrangements. As always, state law varies so the option to levy fees like this may not be available to you. Finally, people in arrears and documented with Family Court where one parent is "in contempt" from not complying with the court may also be treated differently.

Assets take many forms and one should not just limit themselves to the search of international and domestic bank accounts. Planes, boats, cars, art, gemstones, cryptocurrency,

Persian rugs, and precious metals are just some examples of hidden assets you might find during your investigation. A true knack for relentlessness and ingenuity will take you far in asset investigations. If you have a leave-no-stone unturned mentality, asset investigations may be right for you.

Corporate Investigation

Corporate investigation usually involves the private investigator looking into contract compliance, liability, background investigation into new partners, employees, clients, and customers, and competitive intelligence activities. Some larger companies have their own in-house investigators able to complete all of these tasks, but most find it better to out-source these activities when required. Contract compliance is very popular for small businesses who have non-compete agreements in place. Lynx assisted a landscaping business to confirm a former employee not only was violating the non-compete agreement he signed by opening up a shop within 10 miles, but he also was gouging current employees.

For this case, Lynx aided in the development of a sting whereby an investigator posed as a new property owner asking for an estimate using a foreclosed home. The former employee gave a written estimate and as a result we identified the employees working for him. This documentation, covert on-scene photographs and video of the subject and his crew, along with the investigator testimony were turned over to the client's attorney to start legal proceedings.

Background investigations are popular with companies when they are hiring key employees. It is important to note that there is a difference between a background check and a background investigation. A background check normally looks at one database and retrieves certain information such as a criminal record. This can't be considered comprehensive, but offers some assurance. However, a background investigation can be comprehensive. One thing your company can do is offer price options for how deep the investigation will go.

Lynx's uppermost background investigation service is analogous to a federal government investigation for a top-secret security clearance. The only difference is that instead of turning over information to an adjudicator to make a clearance determination decision, it is turned over to the business owner, board, or c-suite executives to make a hiring decision. Verse yourself in private investigator law and make your life easier by getting consent on certain things to maintain compliance with laws such as the Fair Credit Reporting Act. You can only do so many actions without consent. Given that the person wants to be employed by the company requesting the service, you normally should not have an issue obtaining consent. This not only protects you from litigation but also protects your corporate client.

Competitive intelligence is a unique field within private investigation whereby the investigative company is brought in to systematically gather data on customers and competitors so the company who is retaining you can make better product and service-based decisions. Competitive intelligence should not be confused with corporate espionage, which is an illegal activity usually involving the theft of proprietary information from a competitor. Competitive intelligence, while not always ethical, is legal. If you are interested in competitive intelligence, there are organizations out there such as Strategic and Competitive Intelligence Professionals (https://www.scip.org) that can provide further information.

Criminal Investigation

Thanks to the media, if one field of private investigation is sensationalized the most, its private investigation involving criminal investigation matters. A criminal investigation merely gathers evidence to document if a crime occurred and who committed it. Rarely are you kidnapped, in a high-speed chase, or being forced to take the hostage shot to save the day. You are more likely to go to a crime scene long after the police have left and when witness memory has faded.

Lynx assisted a woman who had a rare coin collection stolen by someone she knew. The police had long given up due to time constraints. If these types of cases don't get to an immediate open/close status, they get relegated to the bottom of the pile. While the perpetrator did not off load the coins near where they were stolen, he attempted to do so near his hometown. A simple pattern of life surveillance identified he was spending time between two different locations. This was something law enforcement could not coordinate given their time and resource constraints.

Private investigators are often hired to supplement police (public sector) investigation when a family has a vested interest in the matter. As the family is usually the one who makes this decision, sometimes the police are helpful, but mostly they aren't. This might be because the detective assigned to the case has limited time to investigate a case before additional case work comes in. It is not uncommon for a police detective to be juggling 20+ criminal cases. How much time do you think is being spent on your matter with this workload?

Additionally, many police officers think they are better than you by virtue of position, even if you have a background far superior to theirs. Furthermore, the police are susceptible to the same wild, imaginary views of what a private investigator is because they watch the same entertainment sources as everyone else. These are the facts of life, and I say this as a federal law enforcement agent who has nothing but respect for local, state, and federal government entities. Law enforcement officers are in one of the few professions that keep society from falling into the abyss. With that said, I have learned over the years that in a private capacity, you simply have to play nice in order to get the results you want, regardless of how you are treated.

In legal proceedings, the defense is most likely to hire you to help dispute a matter. When a family hires you, they are banking on the fact you will work a case to completion. Unlike law enforcement, who has a mandate to investigate criminal matters, but not a mandate on how much time they spend on a case, you can do this because you can control your case load. Families will also hire you because they don't trust the police. Years ago, when I was at the Criminal Investigator Training Program at the Federal Law Enforcement Training Center in Glynco, Georgia, one of our topics was courtroom testimony. The instructor specifically told us to highlight our military service and minimize law enforcement accomplishments. Why? Sadly, this is because many people hold the military in high regard but have great disdain for law enforcement. This is something that can help you as a private investigator.

You do not need experience as a police detective to be successful as a private sector criminal investigator, but it certainly helps. You can gather the foundational skills you need by attending an evidence handling course through one of the numerous providers such as at a college where you can earn a certificate in crime scene investigation. One example is the University of California Riverside (I have no affiliation to this program; I just hear good things). Other skills such as physical surveillance, investigative interviewing, database research, and report writing can all be gained at Lynx Criminal Justice Academy or numerous other private sector courses.

Cyber Investigation

Science Technology, Engineering, and Mathematics, better known as STEM, and technology as a whole, continue to be hot career field choices. We are in the middle of the information age and anyone with an advanced knowledge of information technology skills can parlay that into serious profit. Experts in computer forensics can easily bill out at $300 to $500 an hour for specialized services. Computers have become ubiquitous and extracting information off of them or analyzing data on social media can easily become someone's niche. Even seven-year-old children have cellular (cell) telephones (phones) now and cell phone forensics is also a career of its own.

Lynx investigated some cyber bullying for a client on behalf of the client's son. Lynx discovered the client's son manufactured the bullying on himself through his cell phone and his laptop. Subsequent investigation of his computer found that he generated the hateful messages sent to him. Local and state law enforcement agencies normally have limited cyber resources or small computer crimes divisions and don't have time to look into something like this in depth. Overall, it is usually in a person or company's best interests to hire a private firm in order to supplement a police investigation into if a data breach occurred and who conducted it.

Naturally, to excel in this field, you will have to establish a baseline education. Certification is the name of the game in information technology. Having the fundamentals such as Security+ or your Certified Ethical Hacker certification will set the foundations for your success and prove your credibility to respective clients. The best thing of all with training in the cyber-realm is that it can easily be done online at your residence on your schedule.

Domestic Investigation

This is the broadest category of investigation for private investigators and the one the public requests the most. This is also my favorite category of investigation because there is no limit to how financially lucrative these cases can be or the crazy cases you can take on. Domestic investigation is a catch-all term for matters relating to personal affairs. These include child custody cases, infidelity, background investigation, stalkers, child abuse, reputation repair, and elder abuse. Many of the categories of investigation discussed previously, and those soon to be discussed, merge into this field.

For clients, you become a powerful ally in these cases. Many are emotional events and you serve as the independent, disinterested, third-party who can testify to matters witnessed. When you take on these cases, you often become a therapist, even though it should not be in nor become your job description. You have to remain empathetic without allowing the matter to cloud your judgement. Lynx had a client that swore the ex-boyfriend and father of the child dropped the baby on the ground during a custody hand-off. She was trying to pursue full custody. It was actually determined he gently placed the baby in the carrier on the ground instead of handing the child to her out of spite. In her mind this was abuse. You must report facts, even if it is not favorable to your client. Believe me, there are plenty of other investigators who will bend the truth so their client hears what they want to hear. Be the outlier.

You have to be careful with infidelity investigations as well. Some people have a propensity towards violence and as the investigator you don't want to be anywhere near that kind of person if it comes to fruition. One of the client intake (See the Client Intake section for more information) questions Lynx asks prospective clients is about their subject's demeanor: "Do they have a history of violence?" This is something to take into consideration. We also ask if the potential subject has spent time in prison, the Intelligence Community, law enforcement, or the military. People with specialized training from the government coupled with emotion or people who spent time in prison who are emotionally charged could be a recipe for disaster. Surveillance tactics have to be changed when it comes to these types of individuals.

Based on experience, it seems women's intuition is genuine. When men have come to Lynx about infidelity matters, they are usually only right about 50 percent of the time. When women come to Lynx, they are right approximately 90 percent of the time. Infidelity affects men and women physically as well. One male client of ours was so worried about his wife cheating, he lost 26 pounds in two weeks. These clients will be your late night and early morning callers if you conduct 24-hour operations. They will want to accompany you on cases, but you must politely decline. Another phenomenon are female clients coming to you when the boyfriend or husband has been given a second or third chance to cease adulterous activities. I don't take any pleasure in asking the prospective client why she is still with him and if our service is right for her. Lynx does not go in with an intention of bleeding a client dry and neither should you. Most of the time, a female client simply wants to confirm if a partner has changed. I have not seen this with male clients.

We also ask if an investigator was hired in the past during client intake. This is because the cheater usually is now paranoid about getting caught and will change their tactics. A female client retained Lynx to see if her fiancé was still cheating. Another investigation company had previously caught him in an elevator by exhibiting public displays of affection with the paramour and he was now paranoid about riding elevators with strangers. Given the hotel was two floors, it was easy to have someone head up the stairs and cut him off at the pass and get the money shot of them going into the hotel room together.

While the movies often show the investigator getting a picture-perfect shot of the man walking out of a hotel room and getting a kiss on the cheek, the reality is you often rely on a preponderance of evidence. Would a reasonable person believe a woman this man just met at a bar that night was now heading to his hotel room to watch a movie?

Similarly, with child custody situations, people's emotions run wild when it comes to infidelity. In these cases, people will swear up and down that a significant other is cheating. When presented with evidence to the contrary they still won't believe it. It works the other way as well. Meaning, when presented with evidence of cheating, they will move into denial and not believe what you are showing them is true.

A word on boyfriend and girlfriends vs. an actual spouse. Be careful when looking into the actions of a boyfriend or girl-friend vs. an actual spouse unless children are involved. Laws vary throughout the different states and your investigative ac-tions may indirectly be crossing into the stalking realm. Work with your legal counsel to ensure you are covered. You have a lot more freedom of movement when it comes to a spouse, especially in communal property states, than a boyfriend/girl-friend. With all of that said, Lynx still assists with background investigations into potential people getting married. Some-times people want to ensure they are not marrying a fraudster, are not walking into a debt ticking time bomb, or ensuring the person they are about to marry is clean of drugs and other undesirable activities. As these investigations can work on the fringes of ethical mores and might put you in compromising situations, always take these cases based on your own ethical guidelines along with what is legal in your state.

Fraud Investigation

A fraud investigation usually is initiated in order to determine if intentional deception, cheating, or stealing has taken place. Embezzlement, "cooking the books", forgery, Ponzi schemes, pyramid schemes, credit card fraud, identity theft, advanced fee schemes, or other nefarious financial related activities are all fraudulent activities that private investigators can investigate. Fraud hurts business and common individuals alike and can result in the loss of millions, even billions of dollars, not to mention embarrassment. A lucrative field in its own right, those with a background in forensic accounting or the aspiration to learn this skill can easily translate it into the private investigation realm to uncover fraud. Accounting, mathematics, and the other foundational skills will prove valuable to you in pursuing fraud investigation.

One of the first cases Lynx handled was to assist a couple who bought into a bogus time share opportunity. The guy did all the basics of creating a shell limited liability company, business bank accounts, establishing a website, and other things to make the company seem legitimate, but there was no time share. Basic accounting techniques to prove what he did along with database research and investigative interviewing were brought together to locate him. He was tracked down to his father's house and served a summons to appear in court. It was here the father explained he had become indigent due to a massive drug binge. The father accepted the process service paperwork and actually showed up in court on his sons' behalf to pay back the wronged family.

The landmark organization in the private sector for fraud is the Association of Certified Fraud Examiners. The organization is comprised of more than 85,000 members worldwide. Members are primarily investigators, attorneys, accountants, and other fraud professionals. If you wish to learn more about fraud investigation, you need look no further. Their Certified Fraud Examiner (CFE) credential is internationally recognized and worth looking into.

Insurance Investigation

Aside from attorneys, one of the largest users of private investigators are insurance companies. Insurance fraud is so widespread it is in a category of its own. Workers' compensation, premise liability aka "slip and fall" cases, rental insurance, and transit fraud are some of the major categories private investigators work. Investigation businesses are set up solely to investigate workers' compensation claims. Insurance companies generally know who has placed a phony claim and will seek to recoup the money they are paying out. People often make it easy for private investigators to document their activities because they lack situational awareness. Further, with the advent of social media, people make it even easier for investigators to document their activities because they put their entire life online in picture and video format.

For example, a man who was supposed to have no use of his right arm. The man appeared in court with a cast on and went to his physician visits on time. His attorney warned him that a private investigator might be dispatched to document his behavior. But when he was not at these mandated appointments, he could easily be seen playing catch with his dog, carrying groceries, and swimming. Despite ample warnings from defense attorneys, people will continue their business, and routinely blab on social media about getting a big payout or not having to work. These cases can be open and shut the same day because most people are oblivious to the activities around them. However, some insurance companies prefer you document several days of nefarious activity so the claimant can't explain their videotaped actions away.

The major advantage to going after workers' compensation cases is that they provide consistent income seven days a week. Using a traditional billing model, it would be easy to build a team of employees up, send them out for work, and have consistent work for them. The disadvantage to workers' compensation cases is that the market is over-saturated with investigation companies trying to do just that. In the early days of Lynx, we helped with some workers' compensation as a sub-contractor, but quickly found domestic work can far exceed the insurance industry average of $600 for an insurance case. An average is just that, an average. I have seen these cases go for as high as $1,000 and as low as $400.

Because of the industry set up, you can't utilize value-based fees as a billing model. You will have a hard time convincing these companies to bring in a team of investigators on difficult claimants to conduct surveillance on because they are so rigid in their pricing structure. As I often say, surveillance is a team sport, but insurance work almost forces you to have surveillance conducted with one investigator. This is because the industry average comes from a cap of financial resources dedicated towards the claimant, and you are sharing a limited pool of money with professionals in the medical and legal fields.

Liability is a major issue for companies, and they are always keen to eliminate any trace of it. Similar to workers' compensation cases, premise liability claims are widespread throughout the insurance world. A simple YouTube search can produce videos of people faking these crimes. To keep publicity to a minimum, larger companies will habitually settle out of court for small amounts. That is what these fraudsters are looking for. But because these fraudsters also target smaller companies, you get called in. Smaller companies don't have the resources to settle for any sum of money with the fraudster, so they want to ensure the claim has merit. The same suite of investigator skills you use in other cases will be needed to verify if the person in question has actually suffered from an accident.

Missing Persons Investigation

A missing persons investigation is an investigation into the whereabouts of a missing individual. People go missing all the time; sometimes it is for nefarious reasons, sometimes simply to start over. These cases can also involve the search for biological parents of people who were adopted, people looking for old flames, bail skips, old military buddies, runaway teens, and adult children who have had issues with their parents. When adopted people get older, they may have questions about who their actual biological parents are. They may want information for medical reasons or to simply know why they were given up. Depending on the state, you may be able to assist. What you have to educate these potential clients on is that there was a reason they were given up for adoption in the first place. It also may not be one the potential client wants to hear. If you can locate the biological parents, you need to get their consent to release information to the client. Again, many potential clients will not want to hear this.

Lynx uses a universal "missing persons clause" in any cases involving the location of people. This is because the person hiring you may have evil intentions for locating this individual. The "missing" person may be missing for a good reason. They could be trying to avoid domestic violence or wanting a fresh start from a stalker ex. Lynx once fielded a call from a person looking for her "uncle". After the procedures were explained and that consent would have to be given, she told us she would find someone else. Who knows if it was her uncle or an old boyfriend she wanted to stalk? Either way, from a liability and ethical stand point, it is a sound business practice to insist on this clause. Something else you must consider is if a restraining order is in effect. A woman called Lynx who didn't know if her boyfriend was out of the hospital or even what hospital he was in. It was odd she knew he was in a hospital but had no further information. We went through the normal client intake question set and discovered the "boyfriend's" family had placed and received an approved restraining order on her. She flat out told us when asked!

Some investigators will discount their fees if a child is missing. That is a business decision only you can make. Sometimes parents will call you with all the information they need to find their child, but what they actually want is a third party to sort things out. One of Lynx's "missing persons" case involved a father searching for his adult daughter. He felt she was going down the wrong path and believed she was stripping at a local strip club. He did not want to go down there himself so he removed himself from the equation. Lynx sent a female investigator, so he felt more comfortable. It basically turned into a therapy session between the female investigator and the "missing" daughter because she believed he had mistreated her. She ultimately denied the consent to us to provide her contact information and whereabouts to her father but not before wasting 30 minutes of the investigator's time on an impromptu therapy session. You don't win every time.

People have a fascination with assisting in the location of those who disappeared mysteriously or under criminal circumstances. If you are interested in missing persons investigations, you will have to become proficient in the art of skip tracing. Skip tracing is a term that originated in the bail enforcement industry. A skip is someone who actually skipped out on bail or a debt and is the person being searched for while the trace is the actions used to locate them. The techniques are the same whether you work in bail enforcement, process service, private investigation, or any of the litany of interconnected fields.

Technical Investigation

While technical methods are used in almost all investigations, the two types of technical investigations discussed here are Technical Surveillance Countermeasures (TSCM), and the use of the polygraph. TSCM is the official government term for a process of systematically checking your environment for technical surveillance devices in order to detect, neutralize, and/or exploit them. Known colloquially and unofficially as "debugging", "bug sweeps", and an array of other names, the process requires a specialized technician using sophisticated electronic equipment to determine the presence of covert audio and video devices. It is possible to get into this field without going to the federal government's Interagency Training Center, which is the federal government's sole TSCM schoolhouse. However, if you are a graduate, you can command a higher fee as opposed to those only trained in the private sector. You will need an understanding of radios, computers, engineering, electronics, and mathematics to establish a firm foundation in this field.

You also will have to learn how to operate specialized equipment used in these cases such as non-linear junction detectors, spectrum analyzers, x-rays, and thermal equipment. Companies (and some individuals) find great value in you being able to perform TSCM sweeps for them. But the secret with TSCM is to focus on countermeasures as opposed to the actual detection of "bugs". There are products you can train on and set up after you educate your clients on them. An example would be a company that is going to discuss proprietary information in a hotel conference room in a foreign country and wants to ensure competitors don't get access to this information. You might set up a device that skews sound coming out of the boardroom so the client can be comfortable talking openly.

Lynx has done TSCM sweeps for the average person as

well, such as people who feel their car or apartment has been bugged. Be warned now about listing TSCM as a service your company will provide. This service will attract more crazy people to your business than any other investigation service. Some people will swear up and down that they have been bugged and be angry you are not capable of finding the bugs (that don't exist). Luckily, the service is expensive enough that even crazy people come to their senses when requesting the service and you don't even end up having to provide it.

Polygraphers use a polygraph machine to elicit confessions to prove or disprove an allegation. The machine they use is often called a "lie detector", but it actually doesn't detect any lies. It merely measures physiological response, and it is up to the polygrapher to elicit a confession after that. Spouses who are convinced the other party is committing infidelity may insist on them taking a "lie detector" test. Other cases usually relate to theft of property or theft of pharmaceutical drugs, mostly narcotics. The Employment Polygraph Protection Act of 1988 put a damper on almost all private sector polygraph operations. Most industries became off-limits as routine polygraph and pre-employment polygraphs became illegal with only a few exceptions. You can still find utility with individuals who consent to testing on a myriad of topics, primarily infidelity. Private sector polygraphers usually charge between $400 and $1,200 for a two to three-hour session, but former federal government polygraphers can charge up to $2,000.

To use a polygraph, you need to be trained at one of the private sector schools or law enforcement schools nationwide, or at the federal government's National Center for Credibility

Assessment at Fort Jackson, South Carolina. The American Polygraph Association is seen as the governing body for private sector polygraph schools and can provide more information on training. Training courses are 400 hours long at a minimum. PEAK Credibility Assessment Training Center in Cape Coral, Florida is an example of one such school. It is owned and operated by Lafayette, a company that makes polygraph machines. Lynx treats polygraphs as à la carte and does not offer polygraph services but contracts with providers that do. Sometimes, it is not necessary to do every single thing in the field.

Chapter 3
Building the Infrastructure

"audentes fortuna juvat"
(Fortune favors the bold)
-Latin Proverb

Decisions

You now have a better understanding of what a private investigator actually is and what they do. It is now time to decide if this is a venture you are ready to pursue as a private investigation business owner. When I started, I was in debt, had little access to working capital, and was a full-time student who had just left active military service. I did not have a storefront, but I had an apartment. I did not have a secretary, fancy gadgets, independent contractors, or employees. What I had was a laptop, cell phone, determination, and creativity. The business became successful through my actions, not a cash input of millions of dollars. This is important to remember as you read this book.

If you take the plunge and become an entrepreneur, it won't be easy. But I can also assure you it will be infinitely more rewarding and lucrative than serving as a field investigator for someone else's company. There is nothing wrong with being a field investigator and many investigators do quite well over a full 20+ year career. But this book is not for them. This is for someone ready to take a calculated risk and start their own private investigation company. Are you ready?

Picking a Business Name

Choosing a business name seems easy, but it can actually make or break your business before you even start. You will probably have too many ideas or no ideas at all. There are two main strategies you can go with to pick a business name. First, you can use your name then add the necessary supporting words after it to denote a professional investigation agency. For example, if your name is John Q. Smith, your company could be called one of the following:

- John Q. Smith & Associates

- Smith Investigations

- Smith Investigations LLC

- Smith Investigative Group

- Smith Investigations Agency

- Smith Detective Agency

Naming a business after yourself is as simple as it gets. Also, as your reputation grows, using your name might become a major advantage, especially as you remain the centerpiece of the business. Other advantages include its personal touch and you might appear first in a directory. When people deal with smaller companies, they appreciate dealing with the number one, something lost over time for most customers as a company grows. When they call Smith Investigations and talk to John Q. Smith, the final decision maker, it puts their mind at ease. If your name is something that starts with the letter "A" it might make it easier for you to appear first in alphabetized directories. Many people are lazy and will only scroll through the letter "A" before picking a number to call.

Some major disadvantages of using your name include name confusion, the company's initials may not look good, it may not inform customers of what the company does, and it may make it difficult to sell the business when it comes time to sell. Let's face it, some people have last names that are difficult to pronounce. My last name Panico routinely gets mispronounced. I will let you ponder how it is pronounced. In fact, even my first name Edward gets butchered because people regularly add an "s" to it, thus turning it into the common last name of Edwards. This was why I opted to use a relatively unused name for my business. Even if your name is suitable, once it's attached to your company and you no longer want to be part of it, the valuation might be affected because you were the centerpiece.

It's important to consider if the company's initials look good. Imagine if you had a private investigation and security company you named Panico Investigation and Security Services. Think about the acronym for that business! Using a generic ending like "& Associates" may not tell people what services you offer. People will most likely the word associate with a law or accounting firm. If you make it too difficult to determine what you do, your company might get overlooked.

Consider all of this when choosing to use your name.

The second strategy is to make an entirely new name and build your brand from that. Big players use this strategy all the time. Amazon, Apple, Boeing, and Verizon are all examples of this. Even some of the relatively new players discussed in this book subscribe to this model such as Bark, Grasshopper, and Thumbtack. If you follow this course, still ensure you tie the name to an investigations style moniker such as:

- Zeusera Investigations
- Zeusera Investigative Alliance
- Zeusera Investigative Group

You can use this strategy primarily to enable unlimited growth, to target big clients who are more comfortable hiring a large firm, and to give you an exit when the time comes. The primary disadvantage comes from marketing, especially when the name is shared with others in different industries. When your name is not tied to your company, there is no limit to how big it can grow. You can cap it by specializing the name to something like Zeusera Asset Investigations, but don't handicap yourself and keep your options open. Some larger companies will not feel comfortable hiring Smith Investigations if the extent of Smith Investigations is one investigator, or if it even appears that way when it's not. Perception is reality after all. When you get bigger and start attracting buyers for a sale, you can divorce yourself from the company. There are some additional overall do's and don'ts to consider when choosing a business name.

Do:

Conduct a thorough Internet search – run Internet searches on multiple search engines such as Google, Bing, DuckDuckGo, and Yahoo to see if the name you are thinking of is taken.

Conduct a domain name search – once you have some name ideas, check various domain purchase websites such as GoDaddy to see if the name has been taken. Be warned, many years ago all the common word names were bought up so you will have to be creative. You also want the .com name and should forgo others such as .net, .biz, .us, etc. The .com still is the king of Internet real estate. Buying the others is a waste of money. Go for the beachfront property and skip the inland swamps.

Conduct a trademark search – this is an important step that is sometimes overlooked. A simple search on http://www.uspto.gov will cover your initial bases. If you think there will be an issue, you can retain the services of a patent and trademark attorney.

Conduct a Secretary of State (SoS) search – consider looking at the state's SoS page you plan to incorporate in to see if the name is already taken. Simply type the state name followed by "secretary of state business search" in your favorite search engine to locate your state's SoS page. Cross reference the name and see if it already exists.

Tell people what you sell – As already mentioned, don't obfuscate what service you are offering. Under one of the main Lynx operating companies are several Doing Business As (DBA) names assigned to it to cover the bases. There is no limit to the amount of DBA's a business can have.

Don't:

Pick a long name – a business name that is too long will get in the way. Names longer than five syllables will be difficult on customers, your marketing ideas, and your employees. Keep it short, clear, and concise.

Pick a name that limits the business growth – as mentioned earlier, Zeusera Investigations is a way better choice than Zeusera Asset Investigations. You may only want to specialize in asset investigations but things change. If you ever want to expand, you will have to do some major reworking of all company property. It is significantly easier to leave room for growth in the beginning.

Use acronyms – I come from a military background. The military is the undisputed leader in acronym use, but acronyms mean different things to different people. It is safer to avoid them and definitely don't select something that resembles a law enforcement or intelligence agency.

Include place names – unless you only plan on operating in one location, avoid these. You would be surprised how many investigation companies use this model.

Get obsessed with Search Engine Optimization (SEO) key word triggers. SEO remains a key concept in business growth. Algorithms change over time, so making a business name predicated on trigger words is not a sound business practice.

I chose a company name over my name primarily because of my last name. I also wanted to grow it beyond just me. I attached a name rooted in symbolism related to the field. Why a lynx? The lynx was chosen to represent my company because of its symbolism. A lynx is a solitary animal but it occasionally travels in small groups. They are elusive, and it is rare to see a lynx in its natural environment. In certain legends, lynxes are known for wisdom and wise counsel. In Native American folklore, lynxes are known for their vision that provides insight as they search for the truth. All of these qualities are incumbent in an investigator or an intelligence and security professional. Weigh the pros and cons of each strategy, make a list, run it by friends and family, and then execute it. One parting tip for you. If all else fails when you're trying to think of a business name, consider a name generator to get the creative juices flowing. Any Internet search engine can direct you to name generators.

Developing a Business Plan

There are two schools of thought when it comes to business plans. The first school is to have one, the second is to not waste any time on one and dive into action. It is up to you to decide which strategy is right for you.

Having a business plan is essential if you are choosing a traditional funding option to start your business. My entrepreneur friend had a plan for a mobile car washing business. When he went to his appointment at the bank, they told him it was an interesting idea but it needed to be converted to paper before they could decide about it. They would not approve financing without a packet of paper to back it. You need to keep the plan short. No one will read or peruse a 300-slide power point presentation even if they say they did. Plans also adjust over time.

You can't effectively pivot your business if you have a laborious monster to constantly update. Use visual aids. Most people are visual learners and it will be easier for them to interpret your plan. When it comes to the plan itself, make sure it is in a logical order and includes an executive summary, company description, overview of market research outlining the competition and customers in the area, your financials, the services offered, the marketing strategy, describes your team, explains how much you are asking for, and provides a conclusion.

• Executive summary – this should be the first topic covered in your business plan and should be kept to a page or less. It is the general overview of everything about to be subsequently discussed in the plan.

• Company description – this should include your mission statement and what your company plans to do. Provide enough content so the audience understands what your company will be all about. Do not use acronyms because they mean different things to different people.

• Market overview – you will need to analyze a typical competitor to see how they operate, what they charge, what services they offer, and then show how you will do it better in the marketing and sales strategy. You also need to explain the total addressable market (TAM) in your area for customers and what the market will support as far as your services go. TAM is the total market demand for your investigation service.

• Services offered – list the services you plan to offer and describe in layman's terms what they are. What will make your company unique? When first starting out, don't try to list every type of investigation, even if you intend to do all of them. When

I first started out, I scared the insurance company by providing a comprehensive list of investigative services I planned to engage in. I had to shorten the service list for them to cover me.

- Marketing strategy – describe how you plan to attract customers, how you plan to grow your business, and what the cost to acquire customers will be. After all, the bank or investor will be concerned with how they get their money back.

- Show your financials – you won't have any since you are just starting. However, you will need to show a budget, and conservative return estimates. Again, if a bank or investor takes a risk on you, they want to know how they plan to get a return.

- Describe your team – identify each team member, their background, their expertise and certifications. I attended a negotiation seminar once and one thing they talked about was the power of legitimacy. This is where those fancy certifications, training courses, and letters behind your name will come in handy.

- Explain how much you are asking for – going over the top will get you nowhere and is unnecessary. In 2021, there are many work arounds for having a lean start up. Show your number and explain how you got them. There is power in numbers. Specific numbers such as $180,029 stimulate action in people more than an even $180,000. Marketers constantly rely on the magic of the numbers five, seven, and nine. This concept shows you are detail oriented and are not playing around with your projection.

- Provide a conclusion – summarize it and attach additional documents in an appendix, like your investigation license.

Having a business plan remains the traditional path of securing funding and officially putting your idea on to paper and into action. But what about the other school of thought? It is entirely possible to eschew the traditional funding route, and bootstrap it. You will still need to do your research on competition, customers, and determine if there is a need for your service. If you are familiar with the famous line from Murphy's Law, "no plan survives first contact intact", then you will understand where I am coming from with a written plan. You instead need to utilize a modified version of a business concept known as velocity.

With velocity, you can pivot quickly if something is not working. Let the market respond and tell you if you need to continue offering that specific investigation service, and how to do it better. Rely on feedback from clients and how you could have done it better for them. Let the client decide what they want from you and why. Is there a need for that service or requirement? When I first started Lynx, I planned to have each client show their marriage certificate to prove they were married before initiating a domestic investigation for them. But I quickly realized most people had no idea where it was nor did they want to expel the effort to bring it to their initial consultation, so I swiftly pivoted from this requirement.

I skipped the initial business plan. I continued to grow Lynx without that foundational document from private investigation into security consulting, and now into training. Buyers that want to purchase your company only appear after a track record of success. In the military, specialized units knock on your door trying to recruit you and get you to try out for their selection program only after you have demonstrated a track record for success. It's not the other way around. Keep this in mind when determining if you will spend time making a business plan.

Company Formation

There are hundreds of articles and books about creating a company. I am not an attorney so you must do your own research and determine the business structure that is right for you. But I can tell you that forming an actual company is key. You need to establish yourself as an actual business and limit liability. It is the first step in protecting your personal assets and legitimizing the service you will offer. The types of businesses you can form for your private investigation business include:

• Sole proprietorship – a sole proprietorship is a business one person owns with no legal or financial distinction between the business and business owner. It is not a legal entity. As soon as you start conducting business, you are automatically a sole proprietor. You can see how this is a potential recipe for disaster from a liability standpoint. There are many private investigators operating as sole proprietors across the U.S. I consider it a ticking time bomb. One misstep and you, not your company, will be sued. While it might be simple for you at tax time and you do have complete control, the risks far outweigh the rewards.

- General partnership – this is similar to a sole proprietorship, but the general partnership encompasses two or more
partners who split profit returns but share personal liability.
If one of your partners messes something up, you can be held
responsible for it. Who wants that albatross around their neck?
I consider a general partnership the worst kind of business
structure.

- Limited partnership – this is similar to a general partnership, except the key word is limited. In this structure, one
partner, the general partner actually runs the business. The
other partner, the limited partner, is a silent partner who does
not partake in managing the business. The general partner has
unlimited liability for the debt, but maximum control in making business decisions. The limited partner has limited liability
up to how much they invested, but don't dictate day-to-day
operations, and effectively serve as a silent partner.

- Limited Liability Partnership (LLP) – Most of the law
firms you deal with will be structured this way. In an LLP, each
partner has limited liability. Typically, only business owners
in professions that require a state license to practice such as
accountants, architects, attorneys, and physicians can form
this structure. Every state restricts this business structure, but
remember your profession will most likely require licensing
as well so it is possible to form this entity depending on your
state. I have only seen a handful of private investigation companies structured this way.

- Corporation – originating in Roman law, a corporation

is legally considered a separate person as a business entity with the purpose of operating for profit. A corporation is owned by shareholders and has a board of directors to oversee company activities. It can issue stock in order to raise capital. It is created by articles of incorporation. In Internal Revenue Service (IRS) code, the two main types of corporations you will encounter will be "S" and "C". A "C" corporation is the default corporation created, can go public, there are no limits to how many shareholders there can be, and no restrictions on the type of owner. An "S" Corporation can't go public, ownership is limited to 100 members, and shareholders with a few exceptions must be U.S. citizens. The dreaded double taxation is the big disadvantage to this model with personal income tax due both on any salary drawn from the corporation and from any dividends received from the corporation.

- Limited Liability Company (LLC) – the LLC is the newest business entity and has origins in the state of Wyoming back in 1977. It is a hybrid of a partnership and corporation and is the most popular way for people to start a business. An LLC is created by articles of organization and is managed by members. It is also subject to fewer regulations than a traditional corporation. LLCs are considered pass-through entities and taxes are passed on from the LLC to the owner's personal tax return. Given its flexibility, liability protection, ease in which you may be taxed as another entity, and minimal effort to establish, the LLC feels like the way to go. Lynx first setup as an LLC and later built upon the foundational LLC with other LLCs. Companies such as Rocket Lawyer and Legal Zoom can help you form your company, all online. However, I recommend you take the time to sit down with an attorney and discuss your business needs. Company formation costs range from $200 to $2,500 but it is worth consulting an attorney to ensure all your ducks are in a row as laws change all the time.

When a corporate entity is formed, it belongs to the state in which you formed it. Since the LLC is so popular, let's use it an as example from now on. If you create an LLC in Colorado, it is a Colorado LLC. You can form a corporate entity in whatever state you want, regardless if you reside in it. There are tax and privacy advantages and disadvantages depending on the state you form in. If you form an LLC in your home state, it is known as a domestic LLC. If you form an LLC in a state other than the one you reside in, it is known as a foreign LLC. This should not be confused with a foreign country's equivalent of an LLC. Many foreign countries have country specific LLCs such as a Panama LLC. The U.S. does not have an overall U.S. LLC.

It is significantly easier in the beginning to use your home state to establish a domestic LLC than it is to use supposed tax saving strategies by incorporating in Nevada, Wyoming, or Delaware. This is because forming your LLC outside of your home state requires you to register that out-of-state LLC as a foreign LLC in your home state. You now have to pay for two of everything. Two LLC fees, two registered agents, and two of any other fees. This is not a position you want to be in, especially if you are bootstrapping everything. When your company starts growing out of one state, it's then worth exploring out-of-state tax saving options.

You will need an operating agreement for your LLC. While not required, having one is a sound business practice. You can create one from a template online, but it's best to get your business attorney to draft one. The operating agreement is a formal document stating things such as ownership percentage of LLC members, how the company will be run, details about company property, and other related tasks. If you are going the corporation route, you will have to make corporate bylaws as opposed to an operating agreement.

You do not have to name your business entity exactly as you intend to operate it. You can use what is called a trade name, also called a "doing business as" or DBA, to get around the registered name for your business. A DBA allows you to call your actual company whatever you want and do business under another name. In theory, you can call your company Red Dolphin Sticker LLC and file a DBA for Smith Investigations. A final note. All corporate entities require ongoing renewal fees but thankfully they are a tax deduction. It's up to you to find out how much and how many there are.

Each state has specific laws and codes that apply to the formation of a business and specifically a private investigation business. A quick Internet search and you can quickly find the information for your state. Do your research, weigh all the options, and speak to an attorney that specializes in corporate formation. Once you complete all these steps, you should have a firm understanding of what business entity is right for you.

Licensing

Depending on where you live and if you plan to have employees, you may hold as many as four licenses: the business license, private investigator business license, your individual private investigator license (occupational licensing), and any of your employee's private investigator licenses (you will serve as their sponsor).

• Business license – this is required in all 50 states and Washington D.C. unless you go the sole proprietorship route, and even then, you still might need one. Conduct an Internet search for your specific states Secretary of State that handles these matters. Every state has a different section that handles this such as Virginia's State Corporation Commission or Washington's Department of Revenue. Each state actually makes it easy to do this all online and many have checklists to help you along the way. After all, you are about to be creating jobs and that means revenue through taxation for them so they will be pleased. You may want to engage the services of your mentor (see the mentor section for more information) if this is your first time starting a business with help navigating this process.

• Private investigator business license – for this, not only do you need a traditional business license, you also need a private investigator centric business license. This is used to sponsor your employees as private investigators in states that require it. The requirements to be a private investigator business owner are usually more stringent than being an actual private investigator. For example, to start a private investigation business in Maryland, they require five years of experience as a private detective (they are called private detectives in Maryland), or five years' experience as a police officer or investigative experience as a detective/investigator. However, to be a private detective in Maryland only requires submitting an application, fingerprints, and passing a criminal background check. Every state has an entity that handles private investigator business licenses such as Virginia's Department of Criminal Justice Services. Some states use law enforcement entities to regulate the private investigation field such as in Maryland with the Maryland State Police or Arizona with the Department of Public Safety. These entities not only regulate the issuance of certain business licensing, they normally regulate the issuance of occupational licenses as well.

• Individual private investigator license – just like your actual business license, this requirement varies in all 50 states and Washington D.C. You will probably find your individual private investigator license listed under the occupational licenses section next to categories like massage therapist and hair stylists. At the time of writing, Alaska, Idaho, Mississippi, South Dakota, and Wyoming did not require state private investigator licenses. Of those five, Wyoming and Alaska levy local requirements on you. Requirements vary from having some sort of education or experience requirement. Some states are more stringent than others. Florida, Georgia, and Virginia require you to take a training course specific to the state. Just like the Secretary of State, the license requirements might further be delegated to another government entity. Just remember, licensure is no assurance of quality, so don't be concerned how many people are licensed in your state.

- Employee private investigator licenses – depending on the state, an employer might have to sponsor the licenses of their employees, especially if they don't have the requisite experience. Some states like Maryland allow you to work for multiple agencies and each of them can levy their own requirements on the employee. Some states like Virginia also have a special category of employee called compliance agents whose sole job is to ensure all applicable laws and regulations are followed in sectors like private investigation. They will have to maintain records of employees and other important documentation.

Licensing is a necessary step for running your private investigation business. I hope they will implement a national private investigation license for all 50 states along with Washington D.C. and all the U.S. territories. Until legislators truly understand what a private investigator can do, this will not happen.

Resident/Registered Agent

Once you have identified your business name, and setup the appropriate company, you have to appoint a resident or registered agent. The name of this position varies from state to state but it serves the same function. The position exists to accept service of process on behalf of your business should legal action be necessary. In most states you can appoint yourself or your business. Most people choose to appoint a third party. Entire businesses are setup just to handle resident agent services and fees range from $50 to $200 a year.

Most attorneys who form business entities offer this service and will usually include it in a bundle involving corporate entity formation. Lynx chose this option because it was easy. Realize that this rather mundane task is still important. Someone must be available to accept the service of process should you be sued. If the necessary paperwork does not get to you, a default judgement may be entered against you causing you much bigger headaches than you need.

Employer Identification Number

You now have a business name, business plan, company formed, and a registered agent picked out. So, what is next? Well, it's now time to take care of Uncle Sam. You must establish an Employer Identification Number or EIN for your business. It is considered the businesses social security number (SSN). It's better to use that as opposed to your own SSN to add another layer of corporate protection for you. It also further legitimizes your business. An EIN is written as 00-0000000 so as not to be confused with an SSN. You will gain access to databases as a private investigation company that allow you to search EINs. You also can reverse an EIN to find out in what state it was filed for, a skill that will come in handy during investigations. You register for an EIN on the IRS website at https://www.irs.gov/businesses/small-businesses-self-employed/apply-for-an-employer-identification-number-ein-online. It is free and surprisingly simple. Don't pay to have a company set one up for you because it is a waste of money.

Getting a DUNS number

While you are working on getting your EIN, consider getting a Data Universal Numbering System or DUNS number. This will help you get business credit in the early stages and is required to do business with the U.S. Government. DUNS numbers are nine digits and regulated by Dun & Bradstreet, a private company that manages a plethora of business-related activities. They are known for their business credit reports. Even if you don't apply, you will get one whether or not you want one. What is unique about business credit reports is that anyone can pull anyone's business credit report, which is unlike personal credit reports. This will be helpful during your investigations. Once your company goes live, you will start getting letters from Dun & Bradstreet in the mail explaining that vendors are checking your credit. Processing times used to be up to 45 days for a DUNS number, but now are one business day. Once you file for one, you don't have to do anything else. Get your DUNS number at https://www.dnb.com/duns-number/get-a-duns.html.

Establishing a Business Bank Account

Once you have corporate documents in hand, at a minimum the articles of organization/incorporation and the EIN, you can apply for a business bank account. You should do this as one of the first things once your company is live. It further serves to delineate your company assets from your personal assets. There are countless banks and credit unions out there offering business banking services. You will have to do your own research and find the one that works for you. I advise you choose a different bank to where you hold personal accounts. This way, you are not tempted to co-mingle funds, and it demarcates between personal and business assets. You should do everything you can to separate business and personal affairs.

When you first fund the business account, you want to consider a notion known as adequate capitalization. Capitalization in this capacity means the owner(s) have put in enough money to get the company off the ground. There is no set amount. This is a key concept because courts have ruled that an inadequately capitalized business may be grounds to "pierce the corporate veil" and allow for personal assets to be targeted. You will need to keep your company adequately capitalized at all times.

Contemplate choosing a community bank or credit union over a traditional large bank. The fees to operate will be minor compared to what the big banks charge. You also might get more personal service as you are not seen as just a number. Don't forget to explore if the bank has online banking. You would be surprised some banks still don't have online banking infrastructure in the year 2021. Amazingly, some business checking accounts do not pay interest, only business savings accounts.

Something else to consider with business bank accounts is how they link to credit card processing machines. Many companies such as Square and Clover have simplified this process. You will have to see if any of these point-of-sale device companies have partnered with your bank in order for you to receive credit and debit card payments in a timely manner. Always ensure you check fees for these devices as well because even though they are tax deductible, they can add up.

Insurance

Your next step in setting up your investigation business will be to seek insurance. This is required in all jurisdictions requiring investigator licensing. Even if it was not required, it is something you would need to get as a sound business practice. What you will quickly realize about insurance and a private investigation business is that despite retaining private investigators for insurance fraud investigations, most insurance companies have no idea what a private investigator does. Most rope you into the security guard services field. Years of neglect by other investigators and their failure to educate the insurance companies led to this.

It is easiest to work with an insurance broker to find companies willing to sponsor your insurance or you can do an Internet search on your own. There are several companies out there such as Conifer, Hiscox, and the Brownyard Group. Some companies are regional so this will all be area dependent which is why I recommend working with an insurance broker. The two main types of insurance you need are general liability insurance, and errors and omissions insurance. When your company grows and you hire employees, you will need worker's compensation insurance and unemployment insurance.

• General liability insurance – at an absolute minimum, you will need general liability insurance. It protects you against lawsuits and other claims. The cost will be based on a range of factors such as your sales estimates, if you are full or part time, how many people work for you, and if you plan to pay in full or in monthly installments. Cost is typically several hundred dollars but varies by company. What also skews the cost of this is if you plan to be an armed private investigator. If you thought the insurance company didn't know what a private investigator did before, wait until you throw firearms into the mix. Policies will normally include a general aggregate amount such as $1,000,000 and a separate each occurrence amount such as $300,000. Policies can be as much as $10,000,000 general aggregate for investigators. Work with your insurance broker to see how much you actually need.

• Errors and omissions (E+O) insurance – this category of insurance covers your company against claims of inadequate work or other negligent actions. It is a type of liability insurance and costs significantly more than general liability insurance but it's worth it. On my first insurance policy, the E+O portion was six times the cost of the general liability portion and that was with bundling. You need E+O insurance if you eventually plan to branch into other areas such as security consulting, but it should be purchased as a sound business practice.

• Workers' compensation insurance – simply put, once your company has three of more employees, you must purchase workers' compensation insurance. Workers' compensation insurance is regulated at the state level. Check your state laws to see if you need it regardless if you just hire one employee. The overall cost of this insurance depends on the state your business is in, your industry, type of work done, how many employees you have, and if you have ever had a claim in before. All insurance costs are a tax deduction, so welcome to other side of the tax equation.

- Unemployment insurance – the onus is on the employer to pay into a state's unemployment fund for unemployment insurance. Check with your state to see what is required on behalf of your company to remain compliant with this.

There is other insurance out there, and every state levies their own detailed requirements. When you look into business licensing and licensing specific to private investigation, you might come across other requirements. There is no reason to go for the bare minimum in insurance if you actually plan to grow. Weigh all your options and pull the trigger.

Business Location

Once you knock out all the administrative formalities, you need to look at where you will conduct business. The adage of location, location, location is true to a certain extent. But with the advent of technology, it is less important in a service business like private investigation. I can't tell you how many cases I have received and closed over the phone (all pre COVID-19) without meeting my client face to face, and from my apartment. Ideally, you should meet your clients, but not all of them want to nor do they have the time. Your job is to make it easier on them. The main places you can actually operate your business include a traditional office, shared workspace, and a home office. Let's look at each of these options.

First, is the traditional office. This is probably where your mind first went when thinking about starting a private investigation business, but don't let that limit you. If you go down this route, put yourself in an attorney or professional office park.

This way, you present a professional image to potential individual clients and have ease of access to attorneys. You will have to sign a commercial lease and this is significantly different to any residential lease you are used to signing. You can negotiate certain terms, especially if you require special features in your office. Understand what the rent actually includes and if you are signing two of the more common leases, a gross, or net lease. The gross lease includes insurance, property tax, utilities, maintenance costs, and other fees while the net lease separates them all. Recognize what spaces in the building and outside the building the lease entitles you to and your responsibilities to those spaces. Do you get use of a parking space just for you? How many are allocated for your clients at any one time? Do you have to shovel the snow outside or does the landlord have a crew for that?

Lease payment types are also different to the traditional residential lease. You might see payment structures based on rent per square foot or a percentage-based lease, but most offices use the square foot method. Rent per square foot is calculated from a formula consisting of:

square foot x rent per square foot = rent per year ÷ 12 = monthly rent

An example would be a 2,100 square foot office at $10/ square foot totaling $21,000 a year or $1,750 a month. Percentage based leases are predicated on a set amount calculated by the landlord and then adding a percentage of your gross income on to that.

Either way, take the time to negotiate favorable terms for

both you and the landlord. What's really cool about leasing commercial real estate is that your payments are fully tax deductible. I suggest leasing until you have a firm footing under you. While leasing or buying commercial real estate is far outside the scope of this book, I know of one entrepreneur who had to move after his lease was up despite being on location for several years. This is because a new tenant paid over cost for the location. If he had owned the building, he never would have had to worry about being forced out after so many years.

If the building is zoned commercial and you end up with 15 or more employees, then your building needs to comply with the Americans with Disabilities Act of 1990. Remember this as your company grows, especially if you live in a more rural area. For commercial real estate, you need a commercial real estate broker as opposed to someone who works with residential properties. A basic Internet search can help you find people in your area. You can also get the process going online by looking at commercial real estate websites. LoopNet is a good website for finding commercial leases online. They include both offices for rent and for sale in your area.

The second business location option is utilizing a shared workspace a.k.a. coworking space, especially when meeting clients in person. You might not want the hassle of leasing a traditional office or you might be working on your business part time at first. Therefore, it might make sense to utilize a shared workspace. These places will usually set you up with an address, mail pickup, use of a conference room, your own office for private consultations, receptionist support, and other amenities that you share with others in a similar situation. It will allow you to network with other start-up entrepreneurs in similar circumstances. It is a logical cost saving measure to utilize this approach before fully committing to a traditional lease of your own.

Many professionals use this environment, including attorneys who were first starting out. Some people look down on shared work space with disdain. But clients won't necessarily care about your location as much as they care about you solving their problems. Don't get me wrong, you can and should use environment to your advantage. Maybe your client is being followed by their spouse's private investigator and you don't want them coming to your office for your mutual safety. Maybe the spouse is violent and you don't want them putting you in danger. In the early days, I met clients at places such as a McDonald's, a pizza restaurant, and a public library. Professional? I did what I had to in order to eliminate friction, protect the client's wishes, and build the brand without bringing them to my apartment. I closed and retained all three of those clients. One was a $4,000 retainer that had additional hours after that retainer balance was expended. Was it worth it? Just keep that in mind if you have an aversion to a shared work space. Two good companies for looking into shared workspace are WeWork and IWG plc (formerly Regus).

The third option to consider is a home office. I know several private investigators who use this option, including when they meet with clients. Some people like the tax and cost saving features of a home office. You won't have to spend several hundred or several thousand dollars a month on a traditional office or shared workspace, and the portion of your home used for the office is tax deductible. You will save substantial time from the commute to and from a traditional office or shared workspace. You can also structure the home office to provide a personal touch some people will appreciate. Just remember you need to keep the residence clean and professional looking at all times. You also can spend more time with family, which is probably one of the main reasons you are looking at crossing over into the entrepreneurial realm.

There are several disadvantages to using the home office approach. First, a home office might be a poor choice for people who have a hard time separating business and other activities. They need to physically be separate from their home or they may begin conducting leisure activities or helping the family. Consider parking options for potential clients as well. Does your property setup allow for it? Another disadvantage is bringing clients into your actual home. There is a certain seedy type of client that will be interested in retaining your services who you may not want to bring into your home. Don't forget about those crazy clients I mentioned earlier either. Let's say someone thinks a man broke into their house in the middle of the night and put a listening device in their tooth. Is that someone you want in your house? Children and pets can get in the way as well. Children are unpredictable and can detract from the professionalism of the environment. Is the client allergic to your dog or cat? Finally, consider legal implications. What happens if the client gets hurt at your house?

Remember, I never met most of my clients in person, which meant my apartment was an attractive office option. Should you desire it, you can always make a hybrid option for a work location such as using a home office for all administrative functions then going to meet clients at the shared workspace. You could also use a virtual office which is simply the amenities like an answering service but with no physical space so you save on overheads. In the early days, I also used a peer's investigations academy office. I taught there and he would let me use the office to meet people face to face. Get creative, eliminate friction, retain the client, and work the case.

Communication

Everyone knows you need a phone for your business. But most people don't know there are a wide variety of phone options. I first started using Grasshopper for Lynx's business phone service when I was a one-man show. However, as Lynx grew, it also allowed for unlimited phone extensions. The service also gave me a 1-800 number for a national feel along with my local office number. 1-800 numbers are still the king of toll-free numbers despite all the other options out there such as 877. Grasshopper has 24/7 support which was supremely beneficial given I had 24-hour operations going. They even recorded my introductory prompt message which gave me a big business feel, even when I was one person. You can get started with Grasshopper at (*) https://grasshopper.o904.net/LSG

There are a ton of conference call options out there as well. In the beginning with Lynx, I also linked up with Free Conference Call to have meetings with fellow investigators, and with clients and their team. I liked it so much I stayed with it. Registering at the site will get you your own conference call line complete with access code and pin. I have never had a client complain about my use of Free Conference Call. Traditional phones and cell phones can call in on the line. I have also had 20 people on the line when I was standardizing a surveillance team along with eight interns riding with the team. Free Conference Call is bare bones compared to Zoom or Skype but you also won't be having long-term conferences with your clients requiring presentations or demonstrative material. Rather, you are providing an update for them on their case or planning an operation with a team.

Not all cell phone plans support this service, and Free Conference Call levies a nominal one cent per minute charge for a person whose phone is not supported. It is still absolutely worth it, especially if you are on a call with a client who paid you $5,000 and it cost you 15 cents to update them for 15 minutes.

Logo

Every company has a logo, and they make some companies instantly recognizable. Going forward, you will need a logo. Depending on who you ask, there are between four and 10 logo types. They include but are not limited to abstract marks, combination marks, emblem logos, letter marks, logotype, mascot logos, pictorial marks, and wordmarks. If you are trying to make a professional investigation company, I feel you only need to concern yourself with the combination mark, emblem logo, and wordmarks.

- combination marks – a combination mark usually combines pictures with letters. Sometimes, the picture and words can be laid out on top of each other each other to create a special image. An example would be Pizza Hut.

- emblem logos – a favorite of schools and government entities, an emblem is a logo comprised of text inside an icon or symbol. The Harley-Davidson logo is an example of an emblem logo.

- wordmarks – a wordmark is a text and font-based logo that states the business name all by itself, usually in fancy font. Canon is one of the many examples of a wordmark.

I don't feel a mascot logo will get the point across for your business. You can engage the services of a graphic designer to create a logo or create it yourself if you are savvy enough. There are a plethora of companies out there such as Fiverr, Freelancer, and Thumbtack that provide these services at a cheaper rate compared to a traditional firm. This is because you might be paired with a fellow entrepreneur working out of their home who has low overheads. Like with everything, experience and competency may vary so do your research and check out some work in their design portfolio before proceeding. You may also look overseas as there are a ton of companies in countries such as India that can create logos. Just make sure they turn over the source files to you through a copyright transfer agreement which indicates an expressed written understanding that you own the logo once the work is completed.

An Indian company created the first logo Lynx currently uses. I think it works well for now but it might eventually change.

Business Cards and Other Promotional Materials

Once you have your logo, you can make all of your promotional materials with anything from business cards to brochures to polo shirts. The direction you want to take the company will dictate what materials you produce. Literally anything can be made today at low cost from stationary to pens, mugs, t-shirts, and Frisbees. Consider the image of your company and which of these marketing materials are appropriate. I would take it easy at first on all the extra stuff unless you plan on making swag bags for conferences. However, I would spend considerable time on crafting a quality business card given the kinds of people you will target.

I would stay away from the flowery design type cards of creative industries like graphic designers and go with the sleek, sophisticated look on a high-quality material such as 16-point cardstock or titanium. Business card design is an art form now and many companies make high-quality products. Take a page out of the Japanese businessman's playbook and make a good card. Look into your local graphic designer for the best design options.

Website

It is 2021. Gone are the days of not having a website. I once read there were over a billion websites and growing out there. You absolutely need one to compete and get your name out there. Some investigation companies like the mystique of minimizing their web and physical presence. I even read an article once about a company that existed in an office park without so much as a sign saying what occurred in the office. While this protects the privacy of your clients, it only works once you have built the brand and you can take advantage of the best advertising of all—word of mouth. In the meantime, get working on your website.

In the old days, one needed to know how to HTML code and manually design their site. Now with services like Bluehost, GoDaddy, and Wix along with the power of WordPress, you can make your own website and be up and running in a few hours. Again, this is a topic that far exceeds the scope of this book, but some key things to know include domain registration, hosting, content creation, and e-mail creation.

• Domain registration – select what domain name to use for your website. As mentioned earlier, go with the .com and forgo any .net, .us, .org, etc. The com stands for commercial, and that's the kind of activities you are engaging in. Of course, you can also have a .com website and not be engaging in commerce. Companies that help you purchase a domain name such as GoDaddy can quickly show you if the name you want is taken. Be advised, certain words such as "consulting" might trigger a domain to cost more so keep that in mind.

• Hosting – a website host makes your website viewable on the Internet. Each website name is actually a bunch of numbers called an Internet Protocol or IP address such as 12.345.67.8. Every website you view actually has one, but you only see the name of the website unless you know what you are looking for. Most companies out there will pair your domain name registration with hosting to make it easy on you unless you specifically want to register the domain through one company and host it through another.

• Content – the meat and potatoes of the website, is where you describe your company and its services. I wrote all the content on Lynx's websites and let my designer actually design the site. It is important you write all of your content at first as well. Only you truly know what services you are offering. There are companies out there who will make content for you, but I learned that just like the insurance companies, they don't truly understand private investigation. It will take a little time to write the content, but it only has to be done once.

• E-mail. I put this in here because many companies have a website, but don't have a company related e-mail for it. You can run a simple search right now and see how many investigation company business owners who use AOL, Yahoo, and Hotmail accounts for their primary business e-mail accounts. It screams amateur and you don't want to be associated with it. Spend the extra couple of bucks and get a company e-mail.

It seems like an unnerving task at first, but once you actually go through the process, you can see how painless it is to set up a website.

Chapter 4
Building the Team

**"Individual commitment to a group effort—
that is what makes a team work, a company
work, a society work, a civilization work."
-Vince Lombardi**

Teamwork

Archimedes once said, "Give me a lever long enough and a fulcrum on which to place it, and I shall move the world." Well, outside of financial leverage, leverage in business is your team. You will have to start divorcing time from money to be successful. In order to do so, you need a team working with you and for you to accomplish tasks as an extension of yourself. Sure, you can and should utilize a concept known as human capital at first. Human capital is about learning a skill you need and executing it yourself. But know that time is limited and you want to use it to put forth your vision and not on mastering every skill needed to run your business. Business, like surveillance, is a team sport. If you have a team, you can exponentially increase your chances of winning. Team members you will need to include but are not limited to are an attorney, accountant, website designer, employees and/or independent contractors, and a mentor. Let's go over each of these.

Attorney

Utilizing the services of a qualified attorney who can serve as your general counsel is critical to the success of your business. You should do some background research on your attorney. Check their licensing, see if they can practice law in multiple states (this will benefit you for business growth and cases that cross state lines), check complaints against them, and see if they are in good standing with the American Bar Association. An attorney that specializes in working corporate law or with entrepreneurs will be your best bet. Review their fees and see if they are commensurate with their experience. Having them draft contracts or rewrite them in favor of you is crucial to the ongoing running of your business. Gauge their experience working with private investigator business owners. You will most likely be required to sign an engagement letter and fund a retainer account for their services.

Don't be alarmed by most attorney's billing structures. They normally bill in six-minute increments (more on this later when we talk about how you should bill). This means that if the billing rate is $250 an hour and you call and talk to them for three minutes and 13 seconds, it rounds up to six minutes and will cost you $25. After some time spent working with your attorney, they might refer you to potential clients. You have to send your attorney their own 1099-MISC based on your business' tax cycle but in accordance with IRS regulations. Lynx's general counsel is Bernie Dietz. Bernie has been with me since the beginning and provides sound legal advice. Licensed in Virginia and Maryland, I have consulted him on a litany of case-related questions to ensure I followed sound business practices. He drafted all of Lynx's initial service documents and formed the first Lynx company for me. You can reach Bernie at Info@ DietzLawFirm.com or 804-290-7990. Let him know Ed Panico referred you.

Accountant

The next member of your team is your Certified Public Accountant (CPA). When you are a traditional W-2 employee for a company, you probably only see an accountant or tax preparer once a year. This is because you have little to talk about because of the way the current U.S. tax structure is set up. You file your annual income tax returns and are done. There are only minimal tax reductions strategies you can follow. However, when you are a business owner, you will at the very least be seeing your accountant four times a year (much more than that when you talk over your tax strategies). There are many other things you can do to reduce your tax burden. This is where the services of a good CPA come in.

You should vet your CPA the way you do your attorney. Check their licensing, check complaints against them, and check their experience working with start-ups or small businesses. Some CPAs have non-CPA preparers working under them who have their work checked by a CPA. Like your attorney, review their fees and see if they are commensurate with their experience. When forming an entity, have both your CPA and attorney in the same meeting to ensure all your bases are covered and your needs are being met for your particular business and financial situation. I recommend getting a local CPA as opposed to a corporate chain when first starting out, so you have a higher probability of getting someone attentive to your needs. Many CPA firms also offer bookkeeping services which will be key to maintaining your payroll when you are first starting off.

Website Designer

While the two most important members of your outside team are your attorney and CPA, you can't overlook the services of a good website designer if you don't want to create the site yourself. Having a professionally made website can definitely provide the initial aesthetic feel that will put clients at ease. Of course, it will be up to you to secure the client as the website is just an advertisement. But if you have an advertisement, why not have a good one? Ensure the designer you select understands the private investigation field even if you have to educate them on it.

They should ask questions to understand the business. When you deal with the artistic realm, it is easy to look at past products created by the designer. Artists and designers have portfolios with their creations in them. In this case, they should have links to other sites they have created or be willing to provide them to you upon request.

You should ask them about their understanding of SEO and other things to help drive traffic to your site. You will also need to ensure your agreement states you own the content once it is created. This includes any domain name they registered for you as well. Also, will they maintain the site for you or are you expected to do so? What ongoing fees are associated with this? You will have to create the actual text on the site detailing your services. It will be difficult to find a designer willing to do this since they don't know your product or services like you do. You could spend as much as $10,000 on a site as page counts grow and other advanced website tools and capabilities are added. You will have to decide if you want to use human capital on this or outsource it.

Employees

Employees will serve as the foundation of your leverage. If you are not using employees or independent contractors, you are not doing it right. You must understand that labor laws have evolved to provide many rights for employees. You must carefully navigate these to ensure you are properly following the laws. Like your attorney, CPA, and web designer, you are responsible for vetting your potential employees. Consider some broad category advice on the following:

• Background investigation – you will want to leave no stone unturned as you are running an investigation company. Personnel who work for you need to be above reproach because they not only represent your company, but they also will represent you and the clients in court if called to testify. Therefore, the whole gamut of testing should be administered before hiring them including, but not limited to, criminal records checks, reference checks, resume qualifications checks, credit history, and driving records. Consider also setting up a urinalysis test to screen for drug use. You may also want to use advanced hiring techniques such as psychological testing.

• Actual hiring – most traditional companies will have the candidate go through an interview with human resources before moving along to go over a salary and other items in a compensation package. You might consider the traditional panel interview, but also supplement it with situational questions as well. Furthermore, you should add some skills based practical exercises to see if the person actually can do the job. For example, build a phony case and have them work through database checks and some physical surveillance. This will weed out people who talk a good game or who look good on paper but actually can't perform. You can find potential employees through the usual mediums such as Indeed or Monster, but this time you will be posting the job request. You can also follow the "build it and they will come" mantra and have a career tabs link on your website. If you put this up, not a week will go by without you getting at least one resume sent to you. There is something very important but too often overlooked that I want to touch on when it comes to talent management. It is well known that the private investigation field is heavily male-dominated. The lack of gender diversity is a shame because there are outstanding female investigators out there able to do the job. In fact, some of the best investigators I have worked with are women. Also, having a physically diverse workforce with investigators of different races, ages, genders, backgrounds and religions is basically a requirement for this field of work and it will allow your team to successfully conduct physical surveillance in a wider variety of environments.

- Laws – when hiring, you must comply with numerous local, state, and federal laws regarding employees. Some of these include the Civil Rights Act of 1964, Equal Pay Act of 1963, Age Discrimination in Employment Act of 1967, Americans with Disabilities Act of 1990, Family Medical Leave Act of 1993, and the Fair Labor Standards Act of 1938. You are also responsible for deducting child support payments from your employees pay. Compliance will be one of your biggest expenses and time eaters with employees. You may want to utilize an employment or labor attorney to help navigate your first hire.

- Training – as an employer, you are responsible for the hiring process and must include any training for the job they might need. You will also have to provide the equipment to do the job. Consider creating a training program to cover the aspects of the job for which you are hiring. If you need help with making a turnkey training program for your staff, you can contact Lynx for help.

It might seem an intimidating task to bring on an employee. But as stated earlier, having multiple extensions of yourself can truly aid in growing your business and generating wealth. Employees work under your control and direction, and you can quickly allocate them to a new case instead of trying to find an independent contractor. People like to be part of something larger than themselves and will take pride in being a member of your team if you provide leadership and a positive work environment. You won't necessarily get that with independent contractors. You must have a steady caseload before you consider bringing employees on. Also, don't forget, you can start employees out part-time first before transitioning them to a full-time status. Overall, providing stability and having dependable employees will build your business.

Independent Contractors

A useful alternative to having employees is using independent contractors. They can be a tremendous resource. Like employees, there are advantages and disadvantages. Future sections in this book are dedicated solely to employees because they are more complicated to deal with, but in this section, I want to hammer home the benefit of using independent contractors when you first start out. At one point, I had over 30 independent contractors signed to Lynx with various specialties. Think about the overhead savings as opposed to someone solely using employees. You will know exactly how much you need to spend on labor and this will be key in helping you grow.

The biggest advantage of using independent contractors is their temporary ability to supplement your company on a single case to help enhance your workload. This also might happen for a period because your employees are task saturated. But when the job is over, it is over, so you can adjust pay accordingly. Using independent contractors is an excellent way to keep overheads down and when you are first starting out. Independent contractors might further limit your liability because they are not your employees and not entitled to certain protections under the law employees are.

Using independent contractors means you might have to pay a little more on the front end but you make it up on the back end. When you are using an independent contractor, you are supposed to be hiring someone with the expertise and equipment to do the job. That is why you pay extra. However, you don't have to worry about payroll taxes, insurance, child support, or other garnishments. You pay them the full amount and the onus is on them to take out taxes and other related expenses. If you plan to remain relatively small, independent contractors can reduce your labor cost by allowing you to operate on a case-by-case basis versus having employees whom you still have to pay, even if no cases are coming in.

As far as using independent contractors goes, there are some disadvantages. The biggest is that you can't control their overall availability. If they are working on another company's case, they will be unavailable to help you. You must also be careful with using independent contractors because if you use them incorrectly, the IRS might reclassify them as employees and subject you to back up withholding tax. The IRS and government prefer employees to independent contractors. You will need a solid independent contractor agreement to bind them to your company contractually for work you need help with. This will be discussed later in the book.

Keep in mind that just like employees, independent contractor performance can vary. It may be difficult to locate dependable independent contractors. Unfortunately, the private investigation field is full of personnel who got their license in a Cracker Jack box and this presents a constant challenge for you to vet them. Building a heat map with a list of ready personnel available will create a pool of excess talent to draw from during work surges.

Mentor

A mentor is someone who has been there and done that before you and can coach you through to avoid the pitfalls of building your business. This often-overlooked team member is critical in your professional development. Some people think they are too good for a mentor. But you should always strive to learn more and be the best you can be. I once sat in on a speech at the Intelligence Center of Excellence where a military general with 40 years' experience said he had a mentor and that one should always have a mentor. With 40 years' experience, you would think he was at the zenith of his career, but he did not think so. If someone with 40 years' experience in their trade thinks a mentor is a good idea, you might want to consider it yourself.

Your mentor can guide you as you develop your business, and you can have more than one. In fact, you might find it better to have one for private investigation and one for business growth. Organizations such as SCORE (founded as Service Corps of Retired Executives) will help match you with a mentor for free. Teaching and advising is one form of giving back under a free market economy and I can't recommend it enough.

When you find an individual you would like as a mentor, do your homework on them. Read their books, blogs, and talk to people in their social circles—you can find connections on their websites and LinkedIn. Arrange to have coffee and do an in-person assessment of them and see if this is someone you want to emulate. Be prepared to give in return once the relationship is established. This can be accomplished through actions such as helping them with something you are good at or referring business their way. Make it a "win win" for both parties. When you have a mentor, you also gain access to their network who bring in their own unique experiences. This is critical in solving a variety of professional problems and could be a saving grace during the start-up period of the business. When enough time passes, I recommend you pay it forward, especially once you become successful in your business venture.

Chapter 5
Building the Back End

"Opportunity is missed by most people because it is dressed in overalls and looks like work."
-Thomas Edison

Sound Business Practices

Sound business practices involve establishing safeguards to minimize loss of clients and liability. You should lay out a plan to cover you in the most common circumstances you could encounter in an issue. For example, having a credit card form that the client signs shows they authorized an investigation on their credit card. They can't come back and say they didn't authorize you to charge the card and initiate a chargeback. Keep sound business practices in mind during your entrepreneurial ventures.

Employee Agreement and Independent Contractor Agreement

When it's time to have an employee or independent contractor sign on the dotted line, it is essential you provide them an ironclad, easy-to-read agreement outlining the scope of the services they will provide for you. You want it to be minimal on the legalese but still cover all necessary laws for your state and necessary federal laws. It is vital an attorney drafts these documents for you. Incur the one-time cost and use the template they make as your shell for future agreements. You need one for employees and one for independent contractors because these are two distinct categories of workers. Have your attorney make agreements with sections and clauses on:

• Scope of work/job description – you should lay out the left and right limits of the assignment or role the person will fill. List the actual position job title, any "chain of command" or who their supervisors are, and how the performance will be measured.

• Compensation/benefits – the most important section for employees and independent contractors alike. Explain how and when they will be compensated and at what rate. Salary terms or an hourly wage should be listed here. Any special employee bonuses such as Christmas bonuses or production bonuses (helping bring in leads to the company for example) can be laid out here. Don't forget holiday or overtime payment amounts. If there are any benefits for your employees such as a 401k or medical and dental insurance plans, list those as well. Remember, you don't give these kinds of benefits to independent contractors. Common fee's in the investigation realm also cover vehicle mileage, reimbursement for expenses such as entry fees, tolls, parking fees, fuel, hotel charges, cell phone usage, traffic tickets, and other third-party charges related to services being provided. Most companies tie vehicle mileage reimbursement to the federal government rate to make it easy. At the time of writing, that rate is 56 cents a mile.

•   Work schedule – the number of hours the employee is expected to work each week should be listed here. You should cover any overtime terms should these hours be exceeded, and what the procedures to request overtime entails. As a private investigation company owner, you and your workers should forget the traditional Monday to Friday 9–5 PM grind. Scheduling hours will be fluid based on the pattern of life of the subject of your investigation. Remember, you have less control over the direction of an independent contractor when it comes to scheduling, but you can tell them the pattern of life hours for surveillance of the subject so they can effectively complete the investigation on your behalf.

•   Confidentiality agreement – you will deal with sensitive personal and professional matters. It's important to detail how your employees and independent contractors will protect the proprietary and sensitive information they will come across in the conduct of their investigation. Despite what the movies say, unless you are working under an attorney's privilege, there is no special private investigator privilege. Regardless, workers should not blab about their casework at all. The confidentiality agreement should not only cover your client's privacy but the workers' exposure to your business systems, proprietary information, and trade secrets. These are invaluable in their own right and you must provide protection for yourself.

•   Probation period – you should outline a probationary period for your employees to see if they are the right fit. This will make it easier to let them go if they are not working out.

Typical private sector employee probation periods are 30, 60, 90, 180, and 365 days. After three months, you should have a pretty good idea if someone is working out or not, but run your probation period however you want.

• Conflict of interest – a conflict of interest clause covers the aspects of the employee's personal life that may affect their work. For example, an employee should not investigate the spouse of a friend. You need to also lay out stipulations about whether they are allowed to perform work for other employers or work on their own business during mandated work hours, or take on a second job with a competitor. This won't apply to any independent contractors you bring on board. You also need to lay out guidelines for reporting conflicts of interest if a situation emerges later on during an investigation or other work matter.

• Non-compete/solicit – non-compete clauses outline that an employee won't leave and start their own company against your company for "x" amount of months/years and within "x" radius from your offices. Due to their restrictive nature, non-compete agreements are no longer popular. In fact, in California, they are only legal during the sale of a business or other rare circumstances. Non-solicit agreements tell the employee or independent contractor they can't induce or attempt to induce any of your company's clients, employees, other independent contractors, customers, or suppliers of your company to leave your company. It is inevitable some people will try to spite you, especially if they leave on unfavorable terms.

• Intellectual property – your employees and independent contractors will make "work products" for you, especially written products as they pertain to the investigation. Written products will have graphic material, photographs, video, their own analysis of the case, etc. Those products belong to your company and you should have a work made for hire or an invention assignment clause in your employee and independent contractor agreements to cover you. If they develop systems or a better way to do things on the time they are on the clock, those should also belong to you as well.

• Use of technology – you should lay out what is considered acceptable personal use of your technology. Common technology use will include web browsing, social media usage, and sending personal e-mails. You can also cover it in the contract to prohibit employees saying negative things about the company through these mediums as well. Take it one step further as a private investigation business owner and remind workers of the confidential nature of cases and that there should be no discussion of them outside official business. Information should always be factual without the investigator's opinion included. This is because a defense attorney can subpoena your technological mediums such as phones and computers and the last thing you want is an e-mail from one investigator calling the subject of an investigation a derogatory name which may lead to the case being thrown out.

• Disputes and termination – it is inevitable that an employee is fired or quits. Will you pay severance? How much notice do they need to give you? What is required of them upon leaving the company and what is required of you? What property can they keep? What is the turn-in procedures for badges, individual investigator license, etc.? Since going to court ends up being very expensive with an employee who has a claim (bogus or not), you might consider a way to avoid court with a dispute resolution clause. Basically, you want to use a professional mediator (non-binding) or arbitrator (binding) as opposed to litigation to get a final resolution on the issue at hand.

This is not an all-encompassing list, but should provide a few ideas to get started on. However, it's best to use an attorney who gets paid to think about things you will never think of which will minimize or eliminate your liability. One final note. Your independent contractor agreement will have significantly less in it because you exercise significantly less control over the person.

Additional Documents for Employees or Independent Contractors

Employees and independent contractors have different forms to fill out when they apply to work for your company. You should have potential employees fill out a job application form with pertinent information on it before they send their resume in. This would have aided you in completing background investigation on them. When it actually comes time to contract them, an employee will need to fill out an IRS form W-4, also known as an Employee's Withholding Certificate. Employees may change their withholding status as often as they want with a W-4 and the onus is on you to stay compliant with it.

Next, employees are required to fill out the United States Citizenship and Immigration form I-9, also known as an Employment Eligibility Verification form. The onus is on the ac employer to ensure you and the employee fill it out. It must be companied by supporting documentation to show the employee is who they say they are and legally allowed to work in the U.S. The required supporting documents are provided in the instructions section of the I-9.

When you employ someone, you also are responsible for registering with the State's New Hire Registration System so child support can be taken out if necessary. The U.S. Department of Health and Human Services provides oversight. See the state information pertaining to this compliance requirement at https://www.acf.hhs.gov/css/resource/state-new-hire-reporting-websites. If you live in a state with a state income tax, you will have to register to pay this. Simply run an Internet search for your state's tax department and sign up.

As an employer, you are responsible for paying into a state unemployment fund for unemployment insurance. This fund complements the federal program discussed later (in the paying taxes section). Run an Internet search for your state's Department of Labor and follow the instructions to remain compliant. If your state has an internal compliance agent section, you need to maintain a bunch of other forms such as the employee's private investigator license, fingerprint card, weapons qualification information, etc.

At the end of the year, you will issue the employee an IRS W-2, also known as a Wage and Tax Statement. The W-2 can be sent in paper form through the mail or digitally if you have a prior written agreement in place to do so. The W-2 must be sent to the employee by 31 January of the following year if the employee made $600.00 or more. Also, it must be sent regardless of the amount made if you withheld any income, social security, or Medicare tax during the tax year. Failure to provide your employees with a W-2 can result in substantial IRS fines.

Now, there are substantial forms, and documentation required for employees. But what about independent contractors? They are much easier to deal with from a compliance standpoint. When you first bring on an independent contractor, all you need is an independent contractor agreement and an IRS form W-9 also known as a Request for Taxpayer Identification Number and Certification. Crazy right? It's significantly easier because the onus is mostly on the independent contractor to handle taxes for themselves. The independent contractor may fill out the W-9 with an EIN instead of an SSN if you are bringing in another investigation company to assist you with a case. Just like with employees, and if the state you are in requires it, make sure you maintain any documents specific to private investigation and a copy of their credentials.

At the end of the tax year, you send an independent contractor a 1099-MISC, not a W-2. Substantial fines apply if you fail to do so. It can be sent in paper form or digitally. If it's the latter, you must have preapproval in writing first. You have to send the 1099-MISC to the independent contractor by 31 January of the following year if they made $600 or more.

Your state may require additional records so ensure you read up on your state law and check with its regulatory body for more information. States like Maryland or New York that make private investigation business owners sponsor their employees are usually the ones with the most hurdles to overcome.

It's kind of overwhelming from a compliance standpoint isn't it? Keep this in mind when people say "tax all the corporations more" or "companies need to pay their fair share". They have no idea the amount of headache there is in running a business. As a small business owner, you will be burdened with these demands more so than large businesses but are still providing people with jobs. Luckily, there are compliance companies, payroll companies, employment attorneys, CPAs, and other support companies to help you navigate the labyrinth. Remember, you are not alone in this and if you build a strong team, they can help you navigate the business world.

Paying Employees, Independent Contractors & Yourself

You have identified the need to use employees and independent contractors, but how do you plan to pay them? You need to establish a payment schedule whether it is weekly or bi-weekly to pay your employees. Anything else and people get put off. Employees are normally salaried or paid an hourly fee contingent upon the payment terms you laid out in their employment agreement. Independent contractors are normally paid half an agreed fee at the start of the assignment and half on completion of it, or all at the end of the assignment. This can happen at an hourly wage or an agreed upon flat rate as laid out in your independent contractor agreement. There is a lot of bookkeeping software out there to help you manage payroll like Quick-Books. Of course, you can also contract it out to companies like Paychex and ADP. Your CPA's firm might offer this service as well. Payroll will be your single largest expense, but it is all tax deductible.

There are many ways to pay your employees and independent contractors. This includes e-checks, direct deposit, cash, and traditional check. E-checks are popular for sending a check to your worker expeditiously and through a digital medium. A traditional check for the pay period has been a staple of the American economy in the private sector for years. It is simple enough to provide these to your worker at the agreed upon pay dates. Cash gets a bad rap because of its associations with nefarious activity as opposed to privacy and if you are operating in a cash business. You are legally allowed to pay your workers in cash, but it is significantly easier to do so through another medium. This is because you can get jammed up with Federal Insurance Contributions Act (FICA) taxes and other withholdings if you don't stay in compliance.

A direct deposit for your employees is the preferred method to pay them. There is a digital bank transaction showing you paid them and you can easily have this outsourced. Have employees sign a direct deposit authorization form so you can submit it to your business bank. Lynx pays employees with direct deposit and independent contractors with Deluxe e-checks. These are so simple—fill out the information online for the person you are writing the check to and either e-mail them a link or send a PDF copy. Despite the way they look, no bank has ever questioned them.

What about paying yourself? There are many options available to pay yourself depending on the structure of your business. This will depend on what legal entity you have set up for your business.

- LLC – there are a couple of different ways to pay yourself from an LLC. First, you can set yourself up as an employee and give yourself a wage or salary. If you are a multiple member LLC, all members have to agree on a salary under a member-managed structure, unless one member is in a managing role through a manager-managed structure. In this case, you can give yourself a salary without doing so for the other members. Second, you could choose to be paid by profit distribution at the end of the year. The percent you get is based on how many members there are and what percentage they own. Third, you can take an owner's draw against profit or projected profit. Fourth, you can identify as an independent contractor and get paid that way. Finally, you may not want to take any money out, but you will still pay income tax on money that came in and either re-invest the profits made by putting them back into the business or keep them as cash reserves.

- Limited partnership – if you are in a limited partnership, you will take an owner's distribution. As the general partner, all your income is considered earned income so certain taxes will apply. As the limited partner, it can be listed as "passive" income and not be subject to FICA or Medicare. You probably did not get into the investigations business to be the limited partner though, because you have little to no say in how the business is run.

- S corporation – for S corporations, you can receive both salary and distributions and it is a key tax reduction strategy to do so. The key term to remember here is reasonable compensation. If you are identified as paying too much in distributions and not enough in salary, the IRS can reclassify a portion of the distribution into wages toward your salary and tack on penalties. The salary is paid to the S corporation owner and subject to the traditional self-employed and employee withholding taxes. Distributions are paid on profits and exempt from the self-employment taxes you pay on the salary.

- C corporation – there are two ways to pay yourself in a C corporation and those are through dividend payments and as an employee. Since you will be running the day-to-day operations of your business, you will fall under the employee hat automatically. Like with the S corporation, the salary paid to yourself as an employee must be considered reasonable compensation. You can also take dividend payments which are not subject to payroll taxes. Be careful when you do because the valuation of your company can change as the amount of equity in the company changes.

You may wish to include other items in compensation packages for employees. These can include, but are not limited to, overtime pay, bonuses, merit pay, stock options, travel allowance, phone allowance, meal allowance, housing allowance, ammunition allowance, fuel allowance, gym membership, life insurance, tuition assistance, and childcare reimbursement. All of these fringe benefits are potentially tax deductible so consult your CPA for more information.

Employee benefits include, but are not limited to, dental insurance, health insurance, vacation, and retirement plans. You are not required to give any of these and when you first start out you should not feel pressured to do so. Consequently, this is why independent contractors remain an attractive option. You may want to work in a tiered structure as employees get seniority at the company to keep them motivated and moving up the corporate ladder. You may want to make an employee become vested by time on the job before you offer them a 401k retirement plan. Also, don't feel pressured to provide benefits because law firms and technology companies do.

For example, I have a friend whose wife is an attorney at an elite law firm. Yes, they provide her a gym in the office, dry cleaning, meals, an in-office masseuse for neck and shoulder massages, and all of these other niceties you would expect. This is not a no-strings attached or an out-of-the-goodness-of-their-heart policy. They want her in the office producing so they eliminate barriers that keep her out of the office. I also might add that she is salaried and they expect her to work over 100 hours a week to remain competitive at her job in order to meet move up or move out policies in place.

Paying Taxes

Are you ready for the best part of being a business owner? Well, it is paying more taxes than you care to imagine all the time. Of course, I am being facetious about it being the best part. What I am not kidding about is the taxes. The county and state where you conduct business will dictate how many taxes you have to pay and on what. For example, the great Commonwealth of Virginia taxes you on the amount of furniture and other equipment you use in the conduct of your business. Yep, the furniture you use. Taxes on business owners come from the county, local, state, and federal level. You also pay taxes quarterly now instead of once a year before 15 April. Look on the bright side though, things you used to regularly do are now tax deductions and tax credits.

When you are an employee, you are responsible for paying 6.2% percent to Social Security and 1.45% to Medicare. Your employer pays the other 6.2% and 1.45% respectively. Remember, you are now the employer so you have to help shoulder half of the 15.3% load to the IRS. However, you can deduct half of these taxes from your overall income taxes. There is also the burden of paying into a federal unemployment fund because of the Federal Unemployment Tax Act. At the time of writing, the tax was 6% on the first $7,000 you paid to each employee whether they are part time, temporary, or full time. You will calculate your tax liability for each payroll, set aside a monetary amount for each payroll, make your payments to the IRS, and finally submit an IRS Form 940 to the IRS annually, which is also known as an Employer's Annual Federal Unemployment Tax Return.

You are eligible to offset this 6% tax by as much as 5.4% in a tax credit if you paid into a state unemployment fund. This will reduce your tax burden down to 0.6%. Which forms do you use to report your income to the IRS? Glad you asked. It depends on your business entity and again, but make sure you consult the appropriate personnel about the following:

• LLC – LLCs are unique because you can elect to have them taxed as sole proprietorships, partnerships, S Corporations, or C Corporations. If you are a single member LLC, you use Form 1040 (Schedule C) as the income flows to your individual return. If you are a multiple member LLC, you use Form 1065. You use Form 1120S for an S Corporation election, and Form 1120 for a C Corporation election.

- Limited partnership – Limited partnerships are not taxed themselves, instead, the partners are taxed through pass-through income. You use Form 1065, also known as a U.S. Return of Partnership Income, to declare this. You also must complete a Schedule K-1, also known as Partner's Share of Income, Deductions, Credits, etc. As the general partner, your income will meet earned income guidelines and you will pay employment taxes (Social Security and Medicare) on it. As the limited partner, your income is not considered earned income so you don't pay employment taxes on it.

- S corporation – remember there is only one corporation, but how it is taxed (S vs. C) is the true difference. With an S corporation election, you will use Form 1120S, also known as a U.S. Income Tax Return, for an S corporation to file your federal return. The S corporation election only taxes you at the personal level, saving you from the dreaded double taxation of the C corporation. You will only pay self-employment taxes on your wages. What you take as a distribution will not be subject to these payroll taxes.

- C corporation – you pay taxes at the corporate tax rate because a C corporation is a separate legal entity. This rate is 21% now (it was previously 35%) thanks to the Tax Cuts and Jobs Act of 2017. You also pay taxes on your personal return from any salary or dividends you get. For C corporations, you file Form 1120, also known as U.S. Corporation Income Tax Return, for the corporation itself.

I already mentioned that there is a substantial amount of taxes to keep track of now that you are a business owner and potentially utilizing employees. The IRS makes things a little easier to satisfy the burden on you for compliance with the creation of the Electronic Federal Tax Payment System (EFTPS). The EFTPS is a free service the U.S. Department of Treasury provides that you can use to pay these taxes. As of 1 January 2011, EFTPS is mandatory for businesses. You can pay estimated taxes (weekly, monthly, or quarterly in the system), self-employment tax, payroll taxes for your employees, and corporate taxes through the system.

Taxes will be a substantial burden and headache. Just remember that as a business owner, you have a significant number of maneuvers available to you in order to reduce your tax burden that regular W-2 employees do not. Spend time with your CPA developing tax reduction strategies for your business. Realize that it's not about what you make, but what you keep. Taxes have the potential to eat away at your labor and productivity if you allow them to. I will leave you in this section with a quote from former Judge Billings Learned Hand. Hand once stated during the appeals case of Gregory v. Helvering 293 U.S. 465 (1935), later a landmark decision on taxes when it got to the Supreme Court, that, "Anyone may so arrange his affairs that his taxes shall be as low as possible; he is not bound to choose that pattern which will best pay the Treasury; there is not even a patriotic duty to increase one's taxes." As a budding entrepreneur, ensure you recall Hand's statement often.

Standard Operating Procedures

When I was in the military I learned about standard operating procedures (SOP). A SOP is a written document outlying how and why someone should complete a specific task. The military adores SOPs, and it makes sense whether you are in the private or public sector. It eliminates the need to keep making the same decisions. It gives you some of your time back while simultaneously establishing standards for handling a problem.

You can use established SOPs to bring a new employee or independent contractor up to speed on the systems and processes of your company. They don't have to be complicated and they don't have to be unnecessarily long. But they need to be step by step and eliminate any chance of deviation to set your personnel up for success. You may also use them to enable your case managers to make decisions and empower them as managers. Your time is valuable. You won't be able to keep growing if you have to micromanage every aspect of your operation all the time.

The first SOP I ever wrote for my business was for report writing. I wanted a highly polished, uniform product for consumption by consumer or court alike. Everyone writes at a different level. Creating a single, high quality standard for employees and independent contractors has reduced the burden on me and my case managers when it comes to correcting an investigator's reports. Always check your state laws and speak with your attorney before producing in-depth SOPs for your employees and independent contractors. Take the time to write SOPs now, so you don't have to do it later.

Employee Handbook

You will need to create an employee handbook as a single repository of information for your employees to reference. It should lay out all the policies and procedures in place for your company. The goal is to minimize vagueness and ensure everyone understands how you want to run the company. There is no one standard for a company employee handbook. You should make a single page Word document for your personnel and ensure they read it by issuing a receipt. Give a copy to them and retain a copy for yourself. This acknowledgement might be key if there is ever a dispute. The employee can't rely on ignorance as a defense. After all, they said they read and understood your policies.

Make sure you leave some wiggle room for future changes as they will occur. Make sure they understand this is an authoritative document but does not serve as a contract for continuous employment, especially if you want at-will employees. Check all laws that may apply to your company and ensure anything mandatory goes in your handbook. You can have a human resource professional or employment attorney draft this for you. If you want to make it yourself, you should have one of those professionals review the document to ensure it covers all your bases. At the very least, you should cover the following:

• Company background – the first section should be a layout of the company mission. You should mention the history of your company, and its vision for the future. You are the captain of the ship and need to guide it right off the bat.

• Orientation and training – orient the employee to the company, its facilities, and what is available. If they have to complete a formal training program, lay the standards out. If you need help to standardize a formal training program for your investigators, call Lynx to help build a turnkey training program.

• Standards of conduct – this section is generally huge and should encompass absenteeism, hours of work, punctuality, work performance, performance reviews, work area neatness, availability for work, court appearance, dress code, employment classification and status, outside employment, recording time worked, breaks, and meal policy.

• Pay and benefits – this is an important section for your employees. Ensure you cover salary vs hourly pay, bonus pay, any benefits eligibility, insurance and insurance continuation upon termination, holidays off and the need to work holidays, Social Security, retirement contributions, overtime, reimbursable expenses, travel expenses, salary and/or wage increases, allowances, and unemployment compensation. You should also lay out the standards for use of a receipt affidavit if the worker cannot obtain a receipt or loses it.

• Communication – setup standards for mandatory meetings, explain workplace monitoring, which vendors to contact for investigative and work-related tasks and problems, and layout your personal e-mail, personal Internet, and personal telephone calls policy while they are at work.

• Human resources – this section covers areas required by law. Include coverage on problem resolution, disciplinary guidelines, employee relations, criminal convictions and activity, sexual harassment, substance abuse, smoking, drug testing, other acts of misconduct, your Equal Employment Opportunity policy, and Workers' Compensation. Something else the government likes to use in human resources law is an open-door policy and suggestions. This simply means any employee has access to you if they have valid concerns. Layout how that looks and get procedures in place before workers come to you with concerns.

• Company property – since you have to provide certain equipment to your employees, make sure you have a section covering company vehicles or employee private vehicle use, use of office equipment, tools, and supplies, and the return of company property when they are terminated. Using a hand receipt system and making employees sign for property will be key when it comes time for them to turn it in.

• Dealing with clients – you need a section detailing client confidentiality and its importance in the investigation's realm. You also want to reinforce solicitation of clients, vendors, etc. from the employee contract they signed.

• Safety – for completeness, lay out a weapons policy, an active shooter policy, and your zero tolerance for workplace violence. Also, detail emergency actions for severe weather and unsafe work conditions such as a fire.

• Supplementary employment section – you need a section laying out policies on employment referrals, employment of relatives, and the rehiring of employees.

• Vacation and leave – of additional importance to employees and required by law should be a section detailing standards with vacation usage and accrual, military leave, medical leave of absence, jury duty, bereavement leave, a family leave of absence, and paternity and maternity leave.

• Unique to investigators – you should detail policies on database searches, especially if you give your employees access to private investigator only databases via their own unique account ID. You also want policies on the use of drones and other technology, making citizen's arrests, use of informants, use of private investigator badges, procedures for displaying private investigator credentials, and working with international investigators or investigators from other companies. You should also include a section on licensing and how you will either pay or reimburse your employee to maintain their licensing required to conduct their job.

• Educational assistance and training – include a section on potential reimbursement or pay for additional continuing education for your employees outside of the mandatory continuing education required for your state. Just like required licensing, you should cover your employees mandatory continuing education expenses.

• Termination – you need a section covering termination and all aspects of it including job abandonment, voluntary resignation, performance-based release, retirement, termination procedures, and a catch-all for other forms of separation.

Independent Contractor Handbook

If you plan to employ independent contractors, you still

should follow sound business practices and produce an independent contractor handbook. Since you don't want to run afoul of any employee vs. independent contractor situations, you should make an entirely separate handbook for your independent contractors. The sections will be smaller as you have way less control over them. Sections should include, but not be limited to:

• Company overall – like with the employee handbook, you should still detail your company's overall mission and values. By proxy, they are still representing your company with their work.

• Orientation – you still should orient the independent contractor to the company management and structure breakdown so they know how it works. You can provide information about other orientation tasks such as access control, parking, and complaint procedures.

• Training – you won't be providing any training because the independent contractor should be fully trained to complete their task.

• Company property – remind them they can't use company equipment to complete their tasks and have to use their own. No use of company cars, office equipment, cameras, etc.

• Policies – many of your policies for categories like anti-discrimination and anti-sexual harassment are universal due to laws in place and will apply to the independent contractor just as they do an employee. If the independent contractor has a complaint, tell them what they can do to send it up the corporate chain.

- Unique to investigators – as the independent contractor can't use your tools, they also won't be able to have user accounts for your company databases.

Required Employee Posters

When you have employees on the books coming to an office, you need to ensure you have the required employee posters displayed in a common area as required by law. These include:

- An OSHA (Occupational Safety and Health Act) poster

- A Fair Labor Standards Act poster

- A Notices to Workers with Disabilities Act/Special Minimum Wage poster

- An Employee Polygraph Protection Act poster

And when you get to 50 or more employees, a Family and Medical Leave Act poster

You have seen these posters before. Walk into any supermarket and you will probably see them in a common area if they are not in an employee break area. The easiest way to get these posters is to order them from the U.S. Department of Labor. Visit the U.S. Department of Labor's website for the latest and greatest on the mandated posters you need to display.

Dress Code

This is mentioned in the employee handbook section as well. When you have a private investigation business, you will want to implement a dress code. You are not running a tech startup where employees are coming in wearing yoga pants or sandals so they can let their creativity flow. You are building a professional investigation company where you will be interfacing with clients, attorneys, and other professionals. Having employees in appropriate business attire at the office is an important image to project. You don't want personnel hanging around in ratty, torn clothing with obscenities on it while you are trying to close a client. Having a suit should be mandatory for any courtroom appearances your employees make.

Your employees and contractors will need clothing for all types of operating environments. Can they easily transition from a casual environment to a professional environment and still blend in? What is your policy on the use of disguise? Dress code in this sense is pretty unique to private investigation and should be outlined in your dress code policy for when they are out in the field. Sometimes the use of cologne and perfume are included in dress code policies, so consider that as well. Bring in your attorney to ensure you are drafting a policy that is not discriminatory and abides by any laws. Have the attorney go over any consequences you want to implement for not abiding by the policy as well. Lay out your dress code policy in your employee handbook so there is no way employees can say they don't understand.

Notary Ability

It is worth having at least yourself and one other person at your company authorized to notarize documents. Why? It saves a trip to your attorney's office, a bank, having a traveling notary come to your office, or having to visit a UPS store. I remember my first private investigation interview. It was not at the office and I typed up the affidavit right there on the spot. However, I didn't have the ability to notarize it. I had to drive over to a UPS store with a witness in tow to get it notarized. It would have been much easier and more professional for me to have the notary ability and save all that headache. Even if you type it for them, you can still notarize the document because it is their statement, and you simply assisted in the preparation and witnessed it for them.

Performance Evaluations

Performance evaluations are something you probably know about in the private sector and definitely in the public sector. You don't do these for your independent contractors. The best performance evaluation is not to hire them for future cases. However, when you bring on employees, that is a different story. You should create an evaluation form that details their performance, how they can improve, and what they can keep doing that was positive. You can use it as a tool for promotions and raises, to let someone go who isn't a good fit for the company.

The frequency of the performance evaluations is up to you. Some companies like them quarterly, others like them semiannually or annually. Regardless, ensure the evaluation is written as opposed to just doing something verbally. Verbal counsel has a place, but it should be written down to make it formal. Don't do your employees a disservice by holding any gripes or complaints about performance until performance evaluation time when they could have had ample time to fix a problem. The goal is to make the organization a better place so you can keep achieving growth.

My main work experience is with the federal government, where the focus of performance evaluations usually has you striving to meet some attributes or core values of that agency. There is also usually a section for potential and what your supervisor could see you doing the future. For the private sector, you should focus on categories such as actual work performance, problem solving and creativity, attendance and reliability, the ability to meet deadlines, teamwork, and innovation. Also, always do your performance evaluations face-to-face and not over e-mail. So much is lost in communication if it just done by e-mail. The evaluations should be one on one. If you need help to craft a performance evaluation report for your company, you may commission the services of a human resources company with expertise in this area, especially if you are only used to doing these from a public sector standpoint.

Services Agreement or Retainer Agreement

While we will talk about the actual client intake process later, you first have to build the agreement document templates they will sign, save for the actual purpose of the investigation. Notice the use of the word agreement and not contract, even though this is a contract between your business and the client. The word contract is very scary for some people. It is much easier to use the word agreement. It helps with closing a client. Keep this agreement to three pages or less. You don't want to scare away potential clients with a boatload of legalese and a 10-page long agreement. After all, paperwork easily intimidates people. It is essential you have your attorney craft this agreement for you initially because they should be on top of the state laws you must abide by. Once built, it can be used repeatedly. When building your agreement, ensure you cover the following sections:

- Agreement terms – who is the agreement between? It should be between your company and the client, not between you and the client. Remember, you want to keep yourself separate from your business.

- Services clause – layout what services you are expected to perform for the client. One of the biggest things clients complain about is that you didn't do what was asked of you, even if you did. Reduce it to writing and detail it in this section. You also might want to detail how it is based on how you conduct the investigation and that may mean bringing on independent contractors to aid you.

- Representation clause – having a representation section is a sound business practice because you want to ensure the person hiring you does not have a restraining order, protection order, injunction, or other legal restraint put on them from the subject of the investigation. If this occurs, you must cease services immediately.

- Compensation clause – you need to detail how you will be compensated for each case you are working on. We will go into this at length later on in the book. You are not tied to one form of compensation. Depending on the case and service, I change pay structure from hourly to flat to value-based to suit the company and client needs.

- Retainer deposit clause – always get your money upfront

and work off the deposit. I know some private investigation business owners who don't require a retainer deposit. This is a big mistake. All it takes is for someone unhappy with a result, regardless of the clause, and they won't want to pay. Whether you plan to use hourly, flat rate, or value-based fees, get the money up front. If you wish, you can extend some credit for large value-based fee jobs through payment terms such as half up front and half upon completion, or half upfront and half within a week or two. You can make your retainer deposits re-fundable or non-refundable. I advise you to make them refundable as it will put people more at ease.

• Reporting clause – some states require investigators provide a written work product. In states that don't require it, some private investigation owners don't want to provide a written work product. This sheer laziness is most likely due to lack of writing experience and fear as opposed to being afraid of discovery by attorneys. There are definitely times you do not want to provide a written product, but you should strive to give your client a written product that includes the videos and photographs pertinent to your investigation.

• Results clause – this is one of the most important clauses in your services agreement. You must educate your client that you are dealing with the human dynamic and so, it is impossible to guarantee a specific result. Think about it for a second. What happens if you have a standard infidelity case where the wife suspects the husband of cheating. She retains you and gives you a specific surveillance window based on his pattern of life. The husband is indeed cheating, but you don't see it during this time period. She later catches him cheating and calls into question your abilities and services. This is why you can't guarantee a specific result. However, you can guarantee the quality of your work and you should do so.

• Disclosure of information and legal clause – you should have a clause detailing the requirements for you to follow all applicable laws. It should also say the client will keep you informed about the investigation and any pertinent information for it, and your company will reciprocate. This is because the best source of information on a subject of investigation will most likely come from the client. If you are working on a domestic case, the husband (client) will know when the wife (subject) is leaving for "the salon" when she is actually going to go cheat or the insurance company (client) will have a copy of the claimant's (subject) medical appointments which can help an investigator establish surveillance at the best time. On your end, clients often complain about not being informed about their investigation status. This section should include verbiage about client interference in the investigation. If they try to conduct their own surveillance or otherwise jeopardize the investigation, you want the ability to terminate the case.

• Indemnity clause – you should have a clause protecting you from the moment you release the information you provide to the client. You have no control over what they will do with that information. You don't want to provide a husband information about the wife cheating only for him to go and kill the wife because her family can come after you as the progenitor of the information provided.

• Termination clause – you should have a clause explaining what you and the client can do to cease services, whether it be successful completion of the services or if they aren't satisfied; either side should be able to break the agreement in cases like this. Make the termination in writing, not oral, so the client can't say they were wronged and didn't know it.

• Warranties clause – sometimes information from databases is simply inaccurate. This could be for a variety of reasons such as a clerk erroneously populating the database or the person purposely putting false information down. It is best for you to ensure you have a clause stating this possibility.

• Legal clauses – you should have clauses covering limitation of liability, attorney fees, waivers, venue choice, etc. This is why you need an attorney to draft your services agreement for you. They will have a much better understanding of the state laws and additional clauses required in any agreements.

As mentioned above (in the Missing Persons Investigations section), if you engage in missing persons investigations, have an addendum covering how you plan to conduct this kind of investigation. It should state that if you find the person the client is looking for, you first must obtain their consent before releasing their contact information to the client. If they don't consent, it should also cover releasing the client's information to the subject of the investigation so they can contact the client at a later date if they change their mind. It should also remind the client of the results clause in the main agreement and that you can never guarantee a specific outcome.

It is possible to eliminate the hand signing of documents in favor of electronic signatures. Courts have recognized the digital signature of documents as being identical to a wet signature. In the end, it can provide a cleaner and quicker way to send your services agreement to clients. If you are interested in such a service, then industry leaders such as DocuSign could be right for you.

Records Retention

One of the banes of your existence in private investigation will be the retention of records relating to your investigations and the retention of compliance documents for all local, state, and federal entities. For case related documents, look into how long you need to keep case files for, if you are allowed to keep digital files, or if you must maintain physical copies of the files as well. The governing state body responsible for issuing your license usually outlines these rules. For employee forms such as those required for them to work under your license, you must also look to the governing body responsible for the oversight. Maintain copies of items such as firearms certification, standard credentials, employee contracts, and I-9 related forms that prove the right to work in the U.S. Some states like New York and New Jersey require you to keep fingerprint cards of employees on file.

In accordance with the U.S. Department of Labor's Wage and Hour Division, there are also requirements to maintain standard employee records such as standard personally identifiable information, hours worked, pay scale, and anything else related to the employees' pay. This is how they maintain your compliance with the Fair Labor Standards Act of 1938. You should know how long to keep these payroll records (three years at the time of writing) and if digital copies are allowed in lieu of physical copies. The IRS has its own record keeping requirements for employee and employer taxes so stay up to date with those as well. Local, state, and federal agencies can audit you at any time, so keeping pristine records is ideal.

Evidence Retention

Apart from traditional record retention is the ability to gather, transport, and store physical and digital evidence. For physical evidence, you must utilize an evidence log, photograph log, and a chain of custody form. You must document everything and do so redundantly. It's vital to get training on the collection of evidence so you won't contaminate it. For physical evidence, the chain of custody form is crucial in proving that any evidence gathered was not tampered with before it is admitted at the court. Lynx modeled its chain of custody forms off of one of the U.S. Government's forms, but you are free to use any format your state allows. Actual storage of physical evidence is up to you. Having it under lock and key will help prove if someone was able to tamper with it while it was in your control. I have one private investigator colleague who turned a climate-controlled storage unit into his own evidence room.

Digital evidence has its own unique challenges and should follow similar guidelines to physical evidence. You also should backup any digital evidence to a secure online storage site or "cloud" to help with your redundancy. The last thing you need is your computer to die, along with the evidence on it. Working with attorneys on your cases should provide evidence from a private sector lens. You must stay up to date with the latest state laws regarding the gathering, transporting, and storage of your evidence.

Company Transportation

Company transportation is a little different in the private investigation realm because your field investigators will actually need vehicles to conduct their investigations. You can either provide the vehicles for them or you can make them use their own vehicles and reimburse them for wear and tear, fuel, and other maintenance essentials. Regardless, the first step in setting up company transportation is to layout a policy listing expectations you have for workers when they drive. This was briefly mentioned in your employee handbook. It should cover things like talking on cell phones or radios while driving, elimination of other distractions such as eating and driving or texting and driving, and listing out requirements for employees to maintain their own insurance if you plan to have them use their own vehicles.

If you plan to provide vehicles to your employees for field investigation, you should setup a system that makes them "take ownership" of the vehicle. Meaning, they should be concerned with the care and cleanliness of the vehicle, especially if it is shared between other field investigators. You need to get a commercial auto insurance policy and make sure your employees are covered as permissible users of the vehicles. If you do, join a fuel card program so it is easy for your employees to refill the vehicles and for you to track the mileage, use, and related expenses. Having a diverse array of vehicles for surveillance is critical. It might be a better course of action for you to provide said vehicles. Obviously, when you start off, this won't be feasible but you can always have them provide their own vehicles.

If you make your employees use their own vehicles, setup a stipend or reimbursement for the vehicle use since its use is in the furtherance of your business. Even if you have a commercial auto insurance policy that covers permissible users, it won't cover the permissible users' vehicles. You should look into an endorsement called Entitled Employees as Insured. This endorsement enables coverage on behalf of employees who use their personal vehicle instead of one of your company vehicles. It kicks in after the employee's personal auto insurance policy is exhausted. This is beneficial because of vicarious liability. In other words, an employee who caused an accident during the course of using their vehicle for company business makes your company vicariously liable for the accident. This is not a good situation to be in.

You also might want to include a company policy about reimbursement for minor traffic offenses such as parking in a no parking area. I know this runs counterproductive to any driver policy listed above. You certainly don't want to encourage bad driving behavior or breaking the law, but it is inevitable your workers will encounter situations where they don't want to get a ticket and miss out on a great photo for the case. Providing reimbursement will eliminate this burden on them when they are making decisions. Make sure they understand it only applies during surveillance activity and not in their personal time or during any other investigative activity.

Equipment List

As an employer, you have to provide your employees equipment to do their job. You don't provide any of this for your independent contractors. Some common equipment you might want to equip your employees with includes:

• Insured automobile – your employees will need this to conduct physical surveillance, investigative interviewing, or other job-related activities. Preferably, it will have tinted windows in accordance with state laws and a neutral or earth tone color. The benign color is important because it will allow their car to blend in with the environment. Eye-catching bright or ostentatious colors are memorable to someone and will make the vehicle easier to spot. Obviously, this is a large expense and most employers put the onus on the employee. You may do this provided you give the employees a stipend for vehicle use and provide a gas card. The insured part goes without saying. Your employees will spend a considerable amount of time outside of the office and that increases the chances for accidents.

• Cellular telephone – this should be a "smart phone" made post 2016, so it is capable of running modern applications. You might be surprised who doesn't have a phone let alone a smart phone. Your employees will constantly be on their phones taking covert video, e-mailing/communicating with their case managers, utilize GPS, and tracking time worked. Again, instead of providing them a phone, you might choose to give them a small stipend towards their phone bill due to the unique requirements you levy on them.

- Wireless Bluetooth headset – having your hands free from your phone will be key to conducting surveillance. Bluetooth was dead for a while, but is making a comeback due to other wearables like Apple AirPods. Providing Bluetooth for your field personnel could greatly increase their chances of conducting good surveillance.

- Two piece suit or equivalent – some employers provide a small one-time stipend so their employees can purchase a suit. As I mentioned earlier, you will be responsible to set the dress code in your office. It goes without saying that business attire belongs in a traditional office environment, but you can run your office however you want.

- Video camcorder – provide your employees with a video camcorder that was manufactured after 2016. It should have the ability to take photos and date/time stamp video/pictures for courtroom testimony purposes. Having GPS included on the camcorder is a plus but not required. Don't provide ancient VHS style camcorders to your employees! (I am kidding, I know you would never do that). Providing employees a digital still camera as a backup is also key. I once spoke to a professional photographer who moonlighted as a private investigator. He highly recommended a digital still camera as your primary capture device as opposed to a camcorder. You will have to weigh the needs based on the mission.

- Covert cameras – put some money into covert camera options as a backup when the traditional camcorder won't suffice. My lead TSCM tech makes a lot of his own equipment because he loves to do so. He usually creates devices from scratch or modifies commercial off the shelf (COTS) items available.

While this is necessary in the Intelligence Community, you do not need to do this to be successful in the private sector. There are plenty of COTS options through companies like BrickHouse Security that can provide you a range of covert options.

• Monopod/tripod – having equipment to stabilize your employee's camcorders will help get high-quality footage for court.

• Computer – you may put the obligation on the investigator and have them provide a computer, but they will need it to write their reports whether or not you provide it. The latest operating system will allow them to use current software. It may surprise you who does not have a personal computer. The computers should be equipped with Microsoft Office Suite 2016 or higher for easy word processing and other basic office tool capabilities.

• GPS trackers – have a few GPS trackers available at your disposal. Check local and state laws before using these. Brick-House Security has a good selection available.

• Handheld compass – This is a nifty tool you should provide to all of your investigators as a backup to their phone when they are doing surveillance. Knowing what cardinal direction someone is traveling in is key. In Lynx reporting, terms like left, right, front, and back are relative to the person doing the describing. Using cardinal directions like north, south, east, and west are absolutes and eliminate confusion.

• Binoculars – sometimes given your surveillance vantage point, you might need a set of binoculars. Ensure you provide a set to personnel doing physical surveillance that are 7x50 or greater. Your employees will appreciate them as a piece of redundancy in their toolkit.

- Tape recorder – A tape recorder is essential for recording statements of witnesses and other sources of information during interviews. It should be handheld so your employee can bring it with them to field interviews. If you are in the office, you can simply setup a camera on a tripod and do the interview that way. Don't forget the consent to record in the states that require it or just ask as a sound business practice.

- Urinal bottle – This often-overlooked piece of equipment is important for investigators on long surveillance who need to relieve themselves. This way they don't give up their position and lose the money shot. Now they could just use an empty bottle, but it is much more hygienic this way. There is a great item called the Pocket John for this. For female field personnel, there are unique items such as the GoGirl to help them hit the mark. These items are inexpensive and your employees will appreciate you care about their basic needs.

- Portable toilet – you may also opt for a portable toilet in case an investigator has to go number two. When I did surveillance for the Intelligence Community, you needed a good reason for going to the bathroom during an operation, particularly number two. One associate of mine had a fondness for KFC chicken buckets for doing number two. Adult diapers work too. I know several investigations companies that allow their employees to break contact to go number two because a cheating spouse is not the same as an international terrorist (depending on who you speak to).

- Office supplies – yep, you are the one who needs to supply employees with this. Consider using a company for purchasing recurring office supplies. Establishing an account with them will lead you towards building business credit and getting Net D terms such as Net 10, 15, 30, 60, etc. Net D is a type of trade credit allowing you to buy supplies now and pay later based on the supplier's terms.

- All in one printer/scanner/copier/fax – at least one is needed for your employees at the office for them to print, scan, copy, and fax documents necessary to run your business.

- Mobile printer – if your employee is out in the field doing an interview and you want them to get something quickly filled out, then you will need a mobile printer. This is a nice to have but not required as you could easily have them come back to the office and write a report.

- Radios – if you don't want to use a cell phone app as a primary communication device for surveillance, you can use handheld radios like Motorola's. They usually come with low-profile ear pieces, one, two, or three wire communications setups, and other discreet surveillance options. The downside is you will have to make an extra effort to keep track of your surveillance log.

This is not an all-encompassing equipment list, but it is something you will need to think about since it is up to you to equip your employees for success.

Chapter 6
Building the Front End

"Don't be afraid to give up the good to go for the great."
-John D. Rockefeller

The Other Hat You Wear

Remember earlier on in this book in the Private Investigation Defined section when I told you that you were not actually in the investigations business, but the fact finding and information business? Well, I am about to let you in on another surprise. While you will be an investigations business owner, you also will have to learn to be a salesperson. Shocking right? It should not be. Everything you do from now on will involve selling. Selling yourself to the client and proving to them you can solve their problem. Selling yourself to the investor or banker so you can raise capital. Selling yourself to your employees you have a solid company for them to work in. Closing a sale for your business will provide you with some euphoria, especially when you close a client and your bank account gets funded. It's truly a good feeling.

Advertising and Marketing

Advertising and marketing are just two of several hundred billion-dollar business categories that gets bigger every year. When you first start out, you will be a far cry from working with the ad men of Madison Avenue, but there are certainly low-cost alternatives you may explore. The name of the game today is online advertising, but you can still benefit from print and other traditional sources as well. To a certain extent, try to model your advertising off a professional services firm such as an attorney or CPA. They don't have mascots or movie theater advertisements. And they don't send SMS messages out with coupons or discount codes on services. Let's go over a few advertising methods you should use:

• Online – online advertising should be the cornerstone of your advertising platform. Google and Facebook easily command virtually all online advertising with their duopoly in this realm. To advertise on Google, you need to set up a free Google Ads account. After that you build individual campaigns by writing your own copy through the art of copywriting. I am not talking about copyright in the sense that you copyright a piece of work you authored. Instead, copywriting is the art of selling through the written word. Look at some YouTube videos or take a course in effective copy. Use trigger words that drive traffic to your site or develop a call to action so the potential client picks up the phone and calls or they leave contact information on your website. When someone clicks on your ad, you pay out of the budget you set. The more you pay, the more click or calls you can expect. Don't expect this to be a panacea though. A poor ad will not lead to conversion and will just end up costing money. There are a multitude of Facebook ads available from image to video to carousel ads. I don't use Facebook or social media to advertise for Lynx, but that does not mean you should not. Remember, I am showing you a way, not the way.

- Print – what do The National Law Journal, The Legal Times, and Law Practice Magazine all have in common? They are magazines attorneys read and where you should put print ads in. You should consider regional magazines as well when first starting out. Anything put out by your Chamber of Commerce or local community will pay dividends for you. Consider your target audience for getting cases. Are you going after domestic investigations? Perhaps a magazine targeting women navigating the divorce process might be helpful to you. Print as a whole is shrinking compared to online advertising, but it still has a luster to the common person, especially the non-millennial and non-Generation Z crowd. Consider writing a short article for one of these magazines and wrap your advertising in that article. Gary Halbert, the Prince of Print, talked about this method as one of the most effective direct sales messages. It is safe to say he knows a thing or two about copywriting. You could also generate greeting letters or media kits and mail them to law firms, insurance companies, and other small businesses. Be warned that even with effective copy, a secretary might throw this in the trash can and it never will make it to your intended audience. This is nothing personal, so please don't take offense. Small businesses and law firms get inundated with offers daily as people compete to sell to them.
- In-person – in the advent of the technology age, getting

out and about is unfortunately becoming a thing of the past. However, pounding the pavement lets people know you are in the community and open for business. Attending Chamber of Commerce, small business owner's events, trade shows, seminars, and conferences are all excellent ways to meet potential clients. There is a certain psychology involved when someone is in your face actually interacting with you as opposed to over an e-mail or text. Think broad such as workers' compensation or insurance conferences and technical trade shows where you might be able to setup a booth or simply go and mingle. Be careful with certain insurance adjusters who simply want you to buy them drinks and have no interest in actually sending business your way.

• Word of mouth – I saved the best for last. The most powerful form of advertising is the word of mouth. When a referral comes from a trusted friend or business associate, you as a consumer are more likely to act on it or use that product or service the friend is recommending. Getting referrals from successful assignments is an art form you need to master. After Lynx successfully closes a case, a case manager or I always ask if the client knows another person or two who would benefit from our service. That potential introduction is powerful beyond measure and can give you a fresh lead with zero acquisition cost. If you go above and beyond for your client, they might do this on their own. Lynx had a client who e-mailed to us saying she would she let her friend know about our impressive service as she was also going through a divorce. The best part of all is that her friend did contact us. Sometimes, it is that simple.

There are countless forms of advertising and marketing out there. You will have to find the secret sauce for your company. Set aside a budget strictly for your online advertising that makes sense based on the cash flow coming in. The best part about advertising is that it is a business tax deduction. Consult your CPA about the benefits of running a business and advertising costs as a tax deduction.

Getting Clients

Not all clients will call and setup an appointment. Nor will they always leave a message in the contact us section of your website. If you are proactive, there are some additional alternatives to getting clients. Let's start with the online mediums of Bark and Thumbtack.

• Bark is an online medium that allows professionals to bid on presenting their service to a customer once the customer submits a quote. The leads are free and you only pay against your credit bank if you think the customer is right for you. Headquartered in the United Kingdom, Bark has expanded to the U.S. I like Bark because customers submitting a quote provide a phone number and e-mail address which you can later use for marketing purposes. You need to understand the limitation on this medium and on Thumbtack. That limitation is people coming to look for cheap services. Price is usually just one vector people buy on, but on these sites, it is the only concern. Unfortunately, this has led to competitor investigation companies driving the price down as they rush to undercut you, ultimately doing other companies a disservice. You can increase your chances of the customer selecting you by completely filling out your profile and being super responsive on leads sent out. While price is of concern there are juicy leads on there. For example, I had a $5,000 retainer come from a Bark lead.

• Thumbtack is similar to Bark and serves as an online medium between professionals and consumers. Thumbtack is headquartered in San Francisco and commands a larger market share than Bark. You also use a credit system and bid on jobs that interest you. There is a lot of crazy stuff on here and people may ask for things that aren't legal as they clearly don't understand what a private investigator is. Remember that people buy on emotion and justify with logic. If you can sell them on your service and make it stand out above the rest, you could overcome the price vector issue on these two platforms. You can use Thumbtack to gauge the average cost of the service you are offering in your specific zip code so use it as a competitive intelligence tool as well. While I have witnessed my share of crazy customers on Thumbtack, I have also had several $3,000 retainers and one that was $10,000.

• Fiverr and other sites – I would stay away from Fiverr when advertising your private investigation service. Fiverr is great for certain services, but private investigation is currently not one of them. If you run a search for private investigation on Fiverr, your will find unlicensed amateurs dabbling around promising "thorough background checks". This is not something you want to be associated with.

Be on the lookout for other sites similar to Bark and Thumbtack as this style of business continues to grow.

Next is getting insurance company clients. For insurance companies, I already spoke about how overcrowded and difficult this field is to get into in the Insurance Investigation section because you have companies undercutting each other and there is a rigid billing nature of companies in the claims business. The competition further enables the secrecy of breaking into this field as investigation companies zealously protect the leads for these clients. However, if you want to proceed into these deep waters, there are a few strategies you can use to succeed.

First, you should forget going after the big players in the insurance realm like Geico and Progressive. These companies have their own in-house investigators working in a section normally called the Special Investigations Unit or Special Investigative Unit (SIU). They don't need your investigation company's help or if they do, they will choose a national investigations company. Instead, you should concentrate your efforts on insurance defense attorneys, self-insured companies, and Third-Party Administrators (TPA).

Insurance defense attorneys are attorneys who specialize in protecting companies from insurance fraudsters. Since the insurance company is their client, it will be rare for them to contact you. However, if you can forge a relationship with them through your in-person advertising by going to meetings and conferences they frequent, you could get on their radar when a case comes across their desk. Self-insured companies are companies that are financially sound enough to cover their own insurance claims. Think Fortune 500 companies like AT&T and Walmart. The person you are going after to solicit work from is the insurance claims manager for these companies. They may also be called the workers' compensation claims manager, claims specialist, or claims compliance administrator.

If you run an Internet search for self-insured companies, for example "Florida self-insured companies", you will normally find them on a state government website. Most states list who these self-insured companies use as their point of contact for claims, including any TPAs contact information. If these companies don't have an internal claims manager, then they will utilize the services of a TPA. TPAs are not insurance companies or self-insured companies and their job is to process insurance claims and other administrative functions for insurance companies and self-insured companies.

Insurance companies have a wide backlogs of claims and it is easier for them to sub-contract case work out. You can find TPAs by running an Internet search for them or by checking the publicly available records of the self-insured companies from your search above. You then need to get on these companies approved vendor list. This could be as simple as submitting an e-mail through a link on their website with your company information. Every TPA company is different, but once you are on their list, they will contact you when they have a case.

I know an experienced investigator in Massachusetts who got his first insurance company client by religiously attending adjuster associations, insurance conferences, and self-insured association meetings and conferences. He offered to do the first case for these personnel for free. Initially, they all said they were happy with the current private investigation company offering services. Finally, he found a TPA annoyed by the lack of results they received from the investigations company they were currently using. You see, TPAs are on the hook to produce results to the self-insured companies just like investigations companies are. So, he did a difficult surveillance follow for free that the current investigations company botched and provided the written report and video footage later that night. They switched over to his company after that and have been with him ever since.

When I first started, I had no attorney contacts. I went around to each law firm in the area and dropped off my media packages with them, although most had secretaries who probably throw most offers in the trash due to the sheer volume of solicitation requests coming in. One law firm had a massive sign on it regarding unwanted solicitation. Another firm had an attorney nice enough to point me to a local entrepreneur club she was a part of. It was there I met an attorney, in less of a sales type environment, who later rang me. If you live in a smaller town, it might be easier to have attorneys directly reach out to you, but I have only met them through client introduction, word of mouth, and at business functions.

The two secrets I later learned to working with attorneys were to blow them out the water on the first case and to make yourself an integral part of the team. If you are personable, communicate with them frequently, and show them you are not an average investigator, they will work with you again. Show them you are working with them and willing to go the extra mile to complete tasks favorable for them. Attorneys, more than any other profession I have seen, depend on referrals, so it is not uncommon for them to pass your name around. As a bonus, you sometimes will be introduced to attorneys by clients when they bring you in on a case. They will remember you for future cases. Attorneys are sometimes working on a limited budget themselves, so to bring you in might be cost-prohibitive despite any results you can bring to the table. You must explain your capabilities to attorneys constantly and show them you are a force multiplier and not a burden. By educating them on your ability to locate and interview witnesses, locate hidden assets, track down missing heirs, and conduct analysis you leave a lasting impression as a helper and not a hinderer.

These are just a few examples of ways to get clients in this field. There are tons of cases out there ready for the taking if you know where to look. You will get people calling you after the first investigations company they hired botched the job. You will get people who have no limit to what they want done and have the budget to back it up. Law firms, insurance companies, small businesses, and private citizens are out there to help. The only limit to finding clients is you and your ability to hustle.

Client Intake Interview

Once you have an appointment scheduled or a potential client calls you on the phone or through another medium, it is time to understand what they want, see if you can provide it, lock them into a services agreement, and get a retainer deposit. First things first, let's discuss some types of potential and signed clients you will come across in this field:

- Adventure – they have seen the movies, read the books, and watched the television shows. They want to hire you and they want to ride shotgun on surveillance. They want to make arrests and conduct their own investigation. However, client involvement can easily jeopardize an investigation. The reason they are hiring you is to get a disinterested, independent, third party involved. Reinforce that with them. Tell them you will do the heavy lifting. Be careful about advising them about specific information such as the hotel the husband is currently at because the next thing you know, they will be at the hotel. Setting expectations during the initial interview and ensuring you have a clause in your services agreement that deals with interference in your investigation will help you deal with this client.

- Affluent – for these clients, money is no object. They are used to getting their way and will throw their weight around through monetary means. Of course, it is nice to have a client that has the means to fund an investigation, but this is a double-edged sword. They will want your personal cell phone number, unencumbered access to you, and threaten to sue or actually sue you if they don't like how things are going (they conveniently forget the results clause in your services agreement). Treat them with the same respect you would any client, but also ensure they realize you are equals, and you set expectations from the beginning. Make sure they understand you can only guarantee the quality of your work and not a specific result.

- Amnesia – once you have this client landed and completed a thorough interview, this client will suddenly contact you with pertinent information they should have provided you in the first place. Your field investigators might be out on surveillance, when suddenly the client calls and tells you she forgot to mention he is out of town this week. You are about to do a service of process when the client calls and nonchalantly mentions she won't be home all day because she is at the beach house. When you deal with the human dynamic, you will see unpredictability is inevitable. All you can do is ensure you conducted a thorough pattern of life interview during the client intake. This client is not to be confused with someone who suddenly learns of pertinent information and wants to inform you to aid their investigation. Valuable information is always welcome. Definitely keep a two-way communications channel open with any client as you should encourage valuable information to come your way.

• Broke – whether or not they are actually broke, this client will come to you with a sob story and ask you to do the case for free or at a discounted rate. They will ask you to do it for their children, because they are getting physically abused, or pro bono as a public good. They might want to barter, offer collateral until they can come up with the rest of the money, or demand a payment plan. I have even heard of sexual services being offered as payment. While the sexual services client has not happened to Lynx yet, I learned of it through some of the seedier investigators out there. Obviously, you don't want to be involved in any illegal activity and it's up to you if you want to accept barter. You are running a business after all. Simply show them your policies, involve law enforcement if necessary (those claiming physical abuse), and get what you're worth before deciding to deal with this kind of client.

- Cheap – this type of potential client is only concerned about one vector relating to the service and that is price. They do not care about the value you can provide them or how much better you are than the competition. Lynx once had a potential client call and the first sentence out of his mouth in a thick New York accent was "How much do you charge?" How can you answer someone like this? You don't even know what the problem is you are supposed to solve! This client will go through their invoice with you ad nauseam and question every charge. Reinforce the value of your service and either take them on or not.

- Difficult – I have an entire section about this later on in the book in the Dealing with Difficult Clients section. When dealing with potentially difficult clients, all you can do is reinforce the value of your services and make sure you have a lot of patience. When they have money, they are even worse to deal with. Remember, you are under no obligation to take on a client. Ask yourself, is the money worth it to deal with this person? You can always save yourself the headache this way.

- Disbelief – this particular client won't believe the results even when you confirm what they wanted you to confirm, or you disproved it. You can get credible footage of public displays of affection with the paramour, turn it over, and the client will tell you that's not him. On the inverse, you can do something like disprove cheating and the client will say you are not trying hard enough! One of our partners told me they were hired to find damning information on a therapist so she could be sued. This was predicated on the client having a bad experience with the therapist. In doing the research, it was found the therapist was exceptional. The therapist was well liked in the community and had stellar online reviews. When all the information was packaged for the client, she told the investigator, "I am not paying you to help her side, I am paying you to help me, you are not looking hard enough." This is why you must have a results clause in your services agreement. You never know what's actually going to satisfy a client.

• Evasive – this particular potential or actual client seems to exist in the insurance world more often than not. They will give you vague information, ask you to do the case, pay, and you will never hear from them again, despite follow-ups. All you can do is the best you can with the information they gave you to work with and document everything.

• Illegal – some potential clients will come to you with a dangerous intent in mind such as assault or even worse. You have an ethical, moral, and legal obligation not to assist these people and to turn them down. A man called Lynx to ask for assistance to circumvent the government background investigation process. Naturally, we alerted the government organization of his behavior. This type of client will particularly come into play with missing persons investigations. This is why a missing persons clause is essential. You do not want to help someone find a domestic violence victim or a stalker find their victim. You don't want to expose someone with a restraining order to the person they are hiding from. Always ensure you thoroughly vet your client and if you receive information during the investigation that changes the situation, terminate the investigation based on your termination clause.

• Know it all – this client exists primarily in the insurance realm. You will meet insurance adjusters who have been around the private investigation business for a while but aren't actually trained investigators. However, they think they know more than you and will try to direct the investigation by dictating the times and dates they want a claimant surveilled. Sometimes they have legitimate information which is helpful, but they often don't and can hinder the investigation. They waste time and money instead of just letting you handle the case from the start. Basically, in the nicest way possible, you need to inform these adjusters that you are the investigator, and they are the adjuster. You welcome any information that can help get the evidence you need, but you don't welcome them telling you how to run your investigation.

• Miracle – this is another client primarily from insurance companies. They give you little to no information and will expect miracles from it. For example, they will tell you to follow a claimant who they provide the wrong description for, lives in a 300-person apartment complex, and has no car. When you request additional support, they say it's not in the budget and that you must figure it out. You can only reiterate expectation management to this type of client and hope for the best.

• Paranoid – these potential clients are a danger to themselves and you. For some reason, the private investigation profession, more than any other, attracts these kinds of people. They will tell you outrageous claims that don't make any sense. One potential client came to Lynx and said his neighbor was gaslighting him. He said every time he left the house this neighbor would break in and do things like re-arrange the dishes, leave the TV on, turn lights on and off, among other things so he would move out. He claimed he found a camera as well. I explained to him simple things we could do such as residential security consulting, TSCM, covert surveillance, or even posting a security guard outside his door. Every solution was shot down. He never actually wanted service. Another client once told me she was being followed by thirty people from the company she was suing. I thought to myself, the only place I have ever seen that kind of surveillance was in the Intelligence Community and if she could pick out the entire team like that, she would need to be recruited by the government immediately. We set her up with executive protection services to prove or disprove the hypothesis of being followed. Even with the evidence shown to her that no one was following her, she said they were still out there. Her husband was more rational about the whole thing, but he could not convince her either. He had hoped that we could. In the end, he got her counseling. When an intake interview starts going south based on wild stories, you can simply tell them you can't help and move on.

- Sophisticated – this client knows what they want, are educated about the market, and need more time to make a decision. Lynx once had a client that asked a litany of questions during an initial telephonic consultation. When we finished speaking, she said, "I will call you back in 48 hours with my decision" and she did. On the call back, she said she spoke with four other companies in the area and she liked our plan the best and appreciated how thorough we were. Never forget you are also being interviewed. When you realize you are dealing with one of these clients, it is best to give them the room they are asking for, and let them come to their own conclusion.

- Time wasters – unfortunately, these people exist and

there is little you can do about them. Sometimes they just want to hear themselves talk or want to use you as a therapist. They make appointments with you and do not show up or they are late. Both actions suck up valuable time you could be using to close an actual client. Lynx once did a telephonic consultation with a potential client. I thought everything was good to go once I e-mailed him the services agreement. However, upon follow-up, I could not get a hold of him. He disappeared like a ghost, never to be heard from again. It was incredibly frustrating. There is one strategy you can implement for people like this: turn your free consultation into a paid consultation with certain contingencies. You make them pay a deposit before meeting you. If they don't show up, you keep the consultation amount as a cancelation fee. If they do show up, and want to proceed, the deposit they gave you is added to the initial retainer so the consultation costs them nothing. If they show up and do not want to proceed, they get their deposit back. Those are just some ideas to play around with.

• Unrealistic expectations – Lynx often gets calls from potential clients about things we can't or won't do such as hacking a spouse's computer or tapping a person's phone to spy on them. Obviously, these are things you can't legally do (save for special exceptions). Lynx once had a telephonic consultation with a woman who started speaking, then suddenly broke down crying. I asked her if everything was OK, and she replied, "Please don't arrest him!" I thought to myself, what are we arresting him for? She also said he was a good man at heart and she did not want us to beat him up too bad! Of course, we don't get paid to beat people up as private investigators. With potential clients like this, you again must set expectations and explain to them the differences between Hollywood and reality.

The time has come. The potential client is either sitting in front of you or they are talking to you on the phone. You must get to the bottom of what the potential client wants and see if you can solve that problem. As Henry Ford once said, you must "look beyond the individual to the cause of his misery". Chasing your wants won't get you anywhere, but solving people's problems and needs will make you infinitely successful. For Lynx's domestic client intakes, I first try to build some light rapport. Then I let the person explain the reason they have contacted us. I let them talk without interruption. If this request is something I deem is legal and ethical that we can support, I roll into a series of questions about either the incident or subject.

I always start with open-ended questions and then transition to the interrogatives. After I finished gathering information, I repeat it back to the client. This eliminates any misunderstandings you may have made and reinforces to the client you understand everything they want. At the end of the interview, I always ask the client how they heard about us. This little piece of information is crucial in helping identify your customer acquisition cost and seeing what advertising and marketing is working and what is not. Here are some questions I ask the client that should serve as a guideline because every problem set is different, and every subject is different:

• Full name – always get their full name, including any suffixes such as Sr., Jr. II, III, IV, and any honorifics and titles that appear as suffixes such as PhD, M.D., Esq. or J.D.

- Alias/nicknames – this is very important for searching outside the confines of a database that has official names. If someone's name is John Jacob Smith and they go by Jack, no private investigator database is going to pick this up. People also use the same alias for online activity and may include it on dating websites and other online handles.

- Maiden name – if a female is sneaking around, they might use their maiden name. Women today also don't always take their husband's name, so it is important to know this tidbit of information if applicable.

- Date of birth – an important piece of personally identifiable information. Do note that people talk about date of births different. A European might give their birthday as 8/3/1980 with the eight being the day, the three being the month of March, and 1980 being the year. Members of the military might write birthdays like this as well or as 08 March 1980. If you have a keen eye you might notice I write my dates like this in this book. Date of births can help you easily differentiate between people with common names while running database checks.

- Place of birth – someone's place of birth may come into play depending on the type of the investigation being conducted such as an adoption case or employee fraud.

- Physical address – the full address of where the subject resides. You will need this piece of information for your pattern of life and as a potential starting point for locating them.

- Any other property physical addresses – some subjects have multiple pieces of property that they own so you will want to know all of those addresses as well.

• Cell phone number – virtually everyone today over the age of 10 has a cell phone. They are useful for running background investigations/checks, utilizing pretexts, and cross-referencing on cell phone bills, among other things. Getting the cell phone number of the subject is also very important.

• Home phone number – many people have eschewed home phones for cell phones only, but they still play an important part in pretexting and skip tracing. Always ask, just in case.

• E-Mail address – useful for social media investigation, background investigation, web scraping of dating websites, and other nefarious online activity. Many people today end up with multiple e-mail addresses for work, personal, and school. Make sure you collect as many as you can to cross-reference later during open source searches.

• SSN and any EINs – the subject's SSN is a critical piece of personally identifiable information you can use to narrow down your subjects in database searches. Don't worry if the client doesn't know, this as it is easily found in databases that private investigators have access to. The same goes for any EINs associated with the subject. These of course will be useful for asset investigations and contract compliance cases.

• Height – this useful piece of physical description is helpful for your field investigators conducting surveillance, especially when they are trying to locate someone in a crowded area. Try to narrow it down to a two-inch range and know that just like the SSN, not everyone will know this exactly.

• Weight – another useful piece of physical description

information that can help your surveillance team out. Try to narrow weight down to a 10-pound range. Like height, weight should be treated as an approximate.

• Race – an important piece of information, especially when trying to differentiate someone online and when you first try to locate the subject.

• Hair – the length, color, and style of hair helps your field surveillance personnel in their investigation.

• Eye color – another physical description factor helpful for personnel in the field. You may one day have the pleasure of following a subject with heterochromia iridium—a condition where both eye colors are not the same.

• Complexion – yet another physical description factor. Dermatologists and people in cosmetology use the Fitzpatrick Scale that breaks skin types into six categories. You shouldn't expect your client to know these categories, but terms like light or dark will do.

• Facial hair – knowing the current status of the length, color, and style of a subject's facial hair is helpful. This is something people commonly change so photographs may not reflect the current facial hair of your subject. Always ask.

• Build – Dr. William Sheldon first introduced the concept of body types in the 1940s that he labeled somatotypes. He created the categories of ectomorphs, mesomorphs, and endomorphs. Just think of those types as small, medium, and large respectively. You shouldn't expect a client to know if the subject is a mesomorph, but you can have them break a person's build down into small, medium or large. Since I ask this as an open-ended question, it is not uncommon for people to use terms like athletic build, swimmer's build, slender, heavyset, or average. You know what all these terms mean. You have heard them your entire life and can relay them appropriately.

- Distinguishing features – this is an overlooked tidbit of information that can prove valuable for your personnel in the field. Does the subject have any scars, disfigurements, birthmarks, tattoos, piercings, amputations or prosthetics that can help identify them? People love to make themselves different and create a signature that may make it easier for you to locate them.

- Occupation – what does the subject do for a living? This can help with pattern of life information and determine a potential type of education they have.

- Place of work – where does the subject work? What company do they work for? To help build a pattern of life, always get a complete work address as well.

- Education – asking about education level determines access to resources and networks, gives potential intelligence, helps with vetting for background investigation, and explains how a subject might react to certain pretexts. Mark Twain once said, "I never let my schooling interfere with my education". These are words to live by and mean that just because someone doesn't have formal education at a university, you shouldn't underestimate them. Likewise, a physician with an M.D. who completed a PhD to conduct medical research might not have a shred of common sense.

- Law enforcement, military, intelligence, government –

even if their current occupation has nothing to do with it, I always ask if the subject ever spent any time in the military, law enforcement, intelligence or government. This is because those who served in this capacity could have received specialized training from these government entities that make it difficult for a private investigation company to conduct an investigation. Knowing this might change the tactics we use. For example, if they have countersurveillance training we may need to use different tactics to avoid detection. Working cases in Maryland, Virginia, or Washington D.C. will find you dealing with a disproportionate amount of people in the Intelligence Community and federal law enforcement.

- Prison time – equally as important as the question above, spending time in prison gives people a chance to hone skills most people won't have and exposes them to a network of criminals. People who have spent time in prison react differently to people in positions of authority.

- Demeanor – always ask the client about the subject's demeanor and how they might act if they were to discover they are under surveillance. Would they be hostile or violent? While it is possible you have no idea how someone would act, some people are known to be quick to anger. Lynx once did some surveillance on a private sector executive protection specialist who had countersurveillance training. One of the field investigators was behind him at a red light when suddenly, he got out of the car, walked up to the investigator's car, and knocked on the window. He demanded to know why he was being followed and was irate about it. The investigator played it cool, pretended not to know what was going on, and told the guy to get back in the car because he was holding up the line. Luckily, this subject didn't make a bigger deal out of it and did get back in the car. We switched the investigator after that to ensure surveillance continued without a hitch. While surveillance continued properly, this client later compromised her own case and had to cancel services after she left her e-mail account open. The subject went through her e-mails and found correspondence between her and us. P.I. services were of no value at that point.

• Ever been under surveillance by a P.I. before – occasionally a client will hire you who has used another private investigator to follow the same subject. Even without a government or prison background, if these subjects know their spouse or someone else used a private investigator to follow them in the past, they may change their tactics if they are still cheating. It also might make them a little more paranoid about being followed when they cheat again.

• Did the client notify the subject they would use a P.I. – sometimes during a heated argument, a client might tell the subject of an investigation that they will hire a private investigator or have already hired one. Not only does this put the thought of an investigator in their head, it also makes it infinitely more difficult for you to do your job. So always ask this question because it might dictate what tactics you will use on the case.

• Has the client ever caught the subject cheating and notified them – this is similar to the question above but worth mentioning to the client. Sometimes, clients have already caught the subject cheating and told them. The subject is on the second or third chance. If they are still cheating, and unfortunately, they usually are, they might have changed their tactics so you also need to adjust appropriately.

• Preferred type of dress – how someone dresses is key for your surveillance personnel to know. It might impact how they will dress and help the team understand what dress codes are applicable for certain locations the subject might frequent.

• Patterns of life – most people are creatures of habit. Knowing what locations the subject frequents and the addresses for those locations will help identify potential locations the subject is at if surveillance loses them. It also might help provide leads if you have not yet located the subject at the start of an investigation.

• Work schedule – knowing the subject's work schedule can help the surveillance team plan their surveillance.

• School schedule – the same goes for knowing their school schedule.

• Home schedule – their home schedule is also important for the reasons stated above, particularly times they are most likely to be home.

• Medical and legal schedule- for insurance investigations, it is helpful to know when your subject is going to a physician's office for treatment or to court.

• Work and recreational vehicle – not everyone has a vehicle and some people have a work and a recreational vehicle. It is important that you ascertain the year, color, make, model, type (sedan, coupe, etc.), transmission (automatic or manual), the number and state of the license plate, and if there is any body damage or distinguishing features to the vehicle such as bumper stickers, tinted windows, fuzzy dice, etc. You must do this for every car, motorcycle, and boat. Of course, having the client provide photos of the subject's vehicles will make your life easier. You may always pull stock photos from the Internet of vehicles to get an idea of what they look like. If the client doesn't have license plate information, you can always pull it from databases to get a better understanding of the vehicle the subject may use.

- Potential leads – this question is usually applicable to missing persons cases and infidelity cases. Sometimes the client already has an idea of who the subject is cheating with or where they might be. This makes your life infinitely easier when you take on the case. Let them provide their theories, even if they don't pan out.

- Others knowledgeable about case – this question is important for cases involving contract compliance or accident investigation. If there are witnesses or other people you can talk to that can help further the case, you will want to get their name and contact information.

- Recent photo – always ask the client for a recent photograph of the subject of the investigation. People change their appearance from time to time and a recent photograph with the physical description information above provides your field investigators the best possible information.

These questions are not a be all and end all, but will help you think about what you need to know. For example, you will have to ask thorough questions about timelines and events surrounding a theft that don't have anything to do with the description of a subject. All the information from the interview will be taken and packaged for your field investigators to use in the conduct of the investigation. The conduct of an interview exceeds the purpose of this book. If you didn't have the luxury that some detectives, criminal investigators, and Intelligence Community personnel did with investigative interview training, then I recommend you seek some out. It will not only help with interviewing witnesses and subjects, but getting the most information out of the client that will make your life easier when you are drafting an investigative plan.

Investigator Privilege

I want to mention legal privilege here and how it fits into a private investigation as you conduct your initial client interview and later your case. There is a movie called *A Walk Among the Tombstones* starring Liam Neeson. In the movie, Neeson plays a former NYPD officer turned unlicensed private investigator. In one scene, the police pickup Neeson and want to know what's going on about a case Neeson is working on. One detective tells him not to use the privilege defense when talking to him.

While this works for Hollywood private investigators, in the real world there is no such thing as a private investigator privilege between an investigator and their client, with one exception. Yes, you will have access to sensitive client information, and yes, you need to keep it confidential, but no, you aren't legally protected and it might be discoverable, unless the client is an attorney.

The only actual privileges that exist in legal parlance that you will encounter are attorney-client privilege, spousal privilege, self-incrimination privilege, medical professional privilege, and clergy-penitent privilege. The one you will encounter the most is attorney-client privilege which protects oral and written communication between a client and an attorney. This privilege was created so a client could speak frankly with their attorney about their case whether they retained the attorney or not. The attorney in turn is free to give sound legal advice based on that information and render the best legal advice they can to the client.

You may also encounter something called work-product doctrine when working under an attorney. This doctrine helps protect materials from discovery by opposing counsel. If the client intends to use the information you acquire for personal use, then it probably doesn't matter about privilege. But if they intend to use it for litigation, you might want to insist they hire you through their attorney to help protect the information you are about to acquire on their behalf. You will figure this out during the initial client intake interview and recommend to the client, based on the information you have available, which is the best route they should choose. Consult with the attorney you are working under to learn more about attorney-client privilege and work-product doctrine.

Accepting Cases

I am a capitalist. I believe in taking care of my fellow man which in turn leads to building wealth. However, I know my limitations and will not simply accept a case because someone contacts me. Similarly, you don't have to take every case that comes across your desk. For example, Lynx once had a potential client call. The woman wanted surveillance for child custody. She requested it at the bus stop where her daughter was being dropped off at and where the ex-husband would be meeting the daughter. Sounds simple enough right? It was, except she called us at 11:57 AM and the bus was supposed to drop her daughter off at 12:15 PM. This again is part of the problem of people not knowing or understanding what we do or how we do it. It wasn't even possible to send someone from the office to the bus stop in time. You can offer services to someone like this only once they understand how you do business and that absurd requests won't be honored.

Another woman once contacted us about trying to find a man she had slept with the night before. She said the number he gave didn't work, but she had great chemistry with him and wanted to get hold of him. Looking from the outside in, it was obvious the guy had gotten what he wanted and did not have any plans to see her in the future. I explained to her as objectively and professionally as possible that it was not a good idea to pursue using a private investigator to locate him. She appreciated me being forthright and told me if she ever needed any service in the future, she would contact me first. I could have just as easily taken her money, found the guy, gotten his consent, and let her walk back into a bad situation. But what good would that have done? People sometimes contact you at their worst, when they are extremely vulnerable. You must do the right thing and balance building your business with having a moral compass.

How and What to Charge

You want to help the client. Everything appears legal and ethical to you and they want to use you. It's all systems go. Then the conversation turns to price and they ask you how much it will cost, and your mind goes blank. You don't want to find yourself in this situation! Do you charge $200 a day plus expenses like Jim Rockford of the television show *The Rockford Files*? After all, adjusted for inflation this is probably closer to $1,000 a day in 2021 dollars which is pretty good. You should have an idea of what you will be charging for each service you are offering before they ask. There are generally three accepted ways to charge a client for your services. Those are hourly rate, flat rate, and value-based fees. Let's explore each of these.

The standard rate people associate with a service-based business is an hourly rate. Quite simply, it charges the client for each hour your company works on their case. This will also be prorated to a certain time increment such as rounded up to 15-minute increments. You may wish to replicate most law firms who charge an hourly rate and charge in six-minute increments. This compensation is calculated by multiplying the applicable rate per hour by the total number of hours worked. For example, if your hourly rate is $100, and you worked 32.3 hours on the case, then the invoice for the labor will be $3,230 (32.3 x 100). How do you determine your hourly rate? You can use the standard business school formula taught around the U.S. You add up labor and overhead, multiply it by a profit percentage you want to make, and then divide by the total hours you plan to work. The various factors are as follows:

- Determine salary rate – pick a starting number that corresponds with how much you want the business to bring in the first year. Let's keep it simple with $100,000.

- Determine overhead – overhead is all the costs of doing business added up. Think of any bill or expense from advertising and marketing to your phone bill. Let's say this is $25,000.

- Determine profit margin – you don't start a business unless you want to make a profit. Think of profit as a reward for offering your services and doing it well. Business schools teach 10 percent to 20 percent as acceptable even though there is no standard. Let's say this is a conservative 10 percent.

- Determine billable hours – many people calculate this off the standard Monday through Friday, eight-hour workday. However, private investigation is anything but standard work hours because you often work on holidays, weekends, early mornings, and late nights. Many people like to use the standard 2,000 or 2,080 hours which comes from 50 (two weeks' vacation) or 52 weeks in a year, respectively. But the number is much more likely to be around 1,500 hours when you start subtract holidays and time spent on other tasks related to growing your business, etc. Let's say this is 1,500 hours.

- Total it up – now you use the formula S+O X P / H = Rate. S is salary, O is overhead, P is profit, and H is hours worked. Therefore, in our example we have 100,000 + 25,000 = 125,000. We take the 125,000 and multiply it by 10 percent for 12,500 and add it onto the 125,000, totaling 137,500. We then take the 137,500 and divide it by 1,500 to get 91.60 which we round up to $95 an hour.

This formula is best for a solo practitioner which we eventually are trying to get away from. If you are using the hourly rate method, the real key is to charge per investigator (employee or independent contractor) at your hourly rate. Some private investigation companies charge a higher rate for the first investigator and then lower the rate for a second or subsequent investigators. Some companies charge for the case manager as well. As you can see, this could end up turning an hourly rate of $95 an hour into $250 an hour.

Alternatively, you may determine your hourly rate by studying the competition through competitive intelligence, asking your mentor, and directly asking your competitors. Every part of the U.S. is different, so every part will support a different hourly rate. I have seen hourly rates ranging from $35 an hour to $400. Whatever your hourly rate, you will subtract it from the retainer deposit you got up front. The biggest drawback to using an hourly rate will come from people who are shopping on price alone. If your rate is too high, you will scare them away to the competition. It doesn't matter if it takes them three times longer; they were sold on the hourly rate.

When you are dealing with an hourly rate, you can't forget about mileage and all the expenses that come about during the case. Many private investigation business owners add a mileage rate to the cost of hiring them. As I mentioned earlier, most companies just tie the mileage rate to the federal mileage rate of 56 cents a mile (2021 rate) and call it a day. This rate fluctuates every year, so check with the IRS for the latest figure. I have never liked mileage because I feel like I am nickel and diming someone, but it has its place in the private investigation business. For other expenses, you would get reimbursed for them at cost. For example, if you are following a subject into a movie theater and the ticket costs $10, this is added to the invoice.

The next way to bill is flat rate. Flat rate billing is simply taking your hourly rate and multiplying it by the estimated hours you think it will take to close the case. You will also add all of your expenses you project from the case as well. You may put a clause in your services agreement that will reimburse an egregious expense that comes up. Flat rate billing is a little more palatable to the client because they know exactly how much their case will cost them, whereas an hourly rate can seem endless. Once you get an idea how long it will take to close a case, you will see the flat rate is a much better option to the hourly rate because it rewards those who are efficient at completing a task.

You don't have to keep a detailed invoice for a flat rate because the client already knows the exact cost. You will find it easier to use flat rates on one-time services such as background investigation, process serving, TSCM, and record retrieval. Courtroom testimony is another popular category that gets turned into a flat rate and is usually higher than your hourly rate when it is incorporated this way. If you ever step into a courtroom, you will quickly see that you are on their time alone (they move at their own pace) so this is more than justified to cover the time wasted there. I have found it much easier to sell team surveillance as a flat rate service as opposed to hourly.

What makes a bottle of water a dollar on the street from

the guy with the cooler standing at the traffic light, two dollars in a vending machine, three dollars at the movie theater, four dollars at the airport, and eight dollars at an amusement park? The answer is the value you place on this product at the time of purchase. That is the essence of value-based fees. Value-based fees are an entirely different concept when it comes to charging a client. They deal with the value you can provide and the return on investment as opposed to trading time for money. It may be overwhelming to talk value-based fees with a potential client especially if you have never dealt with them before, but they have the potential to exponentially transform the amount of money you can make. Since you can't guarantee a specific result, this will run counter to your agreement (which you will have to modify) and you will constantly have to determine if you can use value-based fees for the client you are talking to. Dr. Alan Weiss is the pioneer in value-based fees, and I highly recommend you learn more about this billing structure. Dr. Weiss has a background in management consulting, but the techniques can absolutely be applied to private investigation.

Some peers can't believe I have pulled off value-based fees from private investigation clients. I can't pull it off with every client as it only seems to work with domestic investigations. If you're successful with an insurance company client using value-based fees, please let me know as I would love to learn from you. One of the most popular draws to value-based fees for your client is they don't have to be afraid to call you because the "meter is running". For you, one of the most popular draws is the exponential fee you can get from your service.

The only way this works is if you can convince the client

you are the best, and only you can get the job done the way they want it. To get started with value-based fees, generate a proposal giving the client at least three different options about how you will proceed with their investigation. People like options. It makes it easier to sell to them and psychologically provides them with the choice and control they crave. You still want them to sign your modified services agreement to legally protect you, but your proposal will lay out the options available to them and the prices associated with those options. Your proposal should include the following categories:

- Client name – list client's name and address.

- Investigation company name – list the company's name and address.

- Scope of work – list exactly what services are expected from you. I also list how and why Lynx is the only company able to complete this assignment.

- Schedule – if the assignment requires a schedule such as surveillance times, list it here.

- Personnel – list the amount of personnel needed for the case and potential backgrounds of those personnel. Be careful to not completely lock yourself in to a specific person, especially if you are using independent contractors.

- Measures of success – layout what a successful case will look like. Notice this is what it will look like and not what it is. You can never guarantee a specific result.

- Payment options – layout at least three different options for service along with the corresponding cost.

- Terms and Conditions – remind the client where the fee rates come from and cover categories such as any expenses and any discounts if they pay in full upfront. When dealing with value-based fees, I extend as much as 50 percent credit depending on who the client is and whether it is the initial job or a recurring one. As in, 50 percent down, 50 percent upon completion or 50 percent down, and the other 50 percent in two weeks on a one-month project.

It might be hard to conceptualize this so here is an example proposal using value-based fees:

- Client – John X

123 Fake Street

Anytown, USA

- Investigation company – ABC Investigations

456 Main Street

Anytown, USA

- Scope of work – Mr. John X, hereinafter Client, is in the middle of a child custody dispute with his ex-wife, Ms. Jane Y, hereinafter Subject. Client's attorney has asked him to gather pattern of life information (at least three instances) of Subject's poor behavior with their child, Jack X, hereinafter Child, so it can be demonstrated to the court. Client would like access to the full suite of investigative services from ABC Investigations, hereinafter ABC. A case manager will be assigned for oversight of the investigation. ABC is managed by current and former Intelligence Officers for the U.S. Federal Government. ABC has assisted clients with numerous child custody cases. All cases have a detailed written investigative report generated. All still and video photography is date/time stamped. All investigators utilized are licensed private investigators in the State of XXXXX and can testify to what they have witnessed during surveillance. While there is never a guarantee of a specific result, the quality of ABC's work is guaranteed.

- Schedule – Client would like ABC to begin work immediately and have options to provide services for as much as possible of a 24/7 period over two weeks.

- Personnel – field investigators have backgrounds ranging from former law enforcement, intelligence, or private sector experience. Any technical installation will be done by technicians who graduated from the Interagency Training Center (ITC) or who have equivalent training/experience. ITC is a federal government facility responsible for training Special Agents and federal Intelligence Officers from across the federal government on technical means. All work is supervised by a case manager to ensure intent is being met within the Scope of Work.

- Payment options:

Option one. Physical surveillance of Subject 12 hours a day, seven days a week, for two weeks. A GPS tracking device will be installed on Subject and Client's jointly registered vehicle to monitor activity during non-physical surveillance hours. Cost for value provided is $XX,XXX.

Option two. All of the services of Option One except that physical surveillance of Subject will be expanded to 24 hours a day, seven days a week, for two weeks. Additionally, social media investigation of Client and all known cyber associates will be conducted to discover any nefarious activity. Cost for value provided is $XX,XXX.

Option three. All of the services from Option Two plus all individuals Subject allows child to come in contact with will receive a background check in order to determine potential reprehensible activity. Cost for value provided is $XX,XXX.

- Measures of success – During the course of two weeks, Subject is documented on at least three occasions demonstrating behavior indicative of poor parenting. Actions include but are not limited to: leaving Child unsupervised for several hours at a time, traveling to known drug areas, utilizing illicit drugs, and associating with individuals committing criminal activity. This information will be turned over to Client and his attorney.

- Terms and conditions –This investigation cannot proceed without the signing of the Services Agreement. The investigation fee is based on the Scope of Work and not on time units. That way you can call us without worrying the "meter is running", and we are free to suggest additional areas of focus without concern about increasing your investment. The fee for the investigation detailed above is paid 50 percent upon commencement of the investigation and 50 percent after the first week of investigation. If you choose to pay the entire amount for the investigation at the outset, you will receive a 10 percent discount on the investigation fee. Expenses such as electronic monitoring equipment, entry fees, tolls, parking fees, and other third-party charges related to services will be billed at cost, separate to the investigation fee. It is payable upon receipt of our statement.

Options are powerful. If you have ever worked in the restaurant industry or car dealerships, or looked at pricing in these establishments as a consumer, you will see options in play. People rarely want to choose the first option, which is your least costly option, for fear of looking cheap. You will also see this with many subscription services provided on the Internet as well. They may list their middle plan as their best seller or their most popular plan even if it is not. You will have to play around with the numbers on the options and ensure you can make an adequate profit and still cover paying your employees and independent contractors.

As your fees for value-based billing might be substantial, I recommend rehearsing telling the client what that number might be so it comes off naturally. For those of you coming from the military, law enforcement, or the Intelligence Community, getting five times your monthly salary for one assignment can be overwhelming, but damn does it feel good to ink that client. You may never feel confident about using value-based fees until you feel like you have mastered your profession.

A word about mastery. There is a story about a woman walking by Picasso in the park as he is painting. She notices it is him and requests he paint a portrait of her. Picasso agrees and paints a magnificent portrait of the woman in a few minutes. The woman is thrilled by the quality of the work and the speed at which it was completed. She asks him how much it costs and he tells her 50,000 French francs. The woman is completely blown away. She tells Picasso that it only took him five minutes to do. Picasso tells her she is wrong. He says it took him his whole life to do. Once you are confident in your chosen profession and have the skills to back it up, you should feel very comfortable charging what you charge and not be concerned about your competitors. So many people in this profession try to undercut each other by offering the lowest prices; it degrades not only themselves, but the ability for anyone to make a living in this field. Private investigation business owners should work to raise the bar, not lower it.

Collecting Payment

When it comes to collecting payment, keep in mind a business concept known as friction. This is basically how difficult it is for a client to buy a product or service from you. Eliminate friction at all costs. Accept all forms of payment you can to remove any friction. For example, some businesses are afraid to handle cash. Put safeguards in place for each payment medium. For example, if the client is paying by credit or debit card, have them fill out a credit/debit card authorization sheet. This way, they can't come back and say they don't recognize the charge on their card. If you get paid in cash, use one of those counterfeit pens to determine if it is legitimate cash.

I don't start on any case until payment clears, especially from a traditional check. If you want a master class in eliminating friction, look at how Amazon turns paying for things on its website into an ice-skating rink with one click ordering. You are primed psychologically to purchase through the advertising of the item and it literally takes one click for them to run your credit card and purchase the item you were looking at.

There are so many pay mediums available today from the

traditional like cash, credit/debit card, check, cashier's check, and money order to the not-so-traditional such as PayPal, Apple Pay, and even crypto-currency. Don't self-eliminate payment options. Some international private investigation companies will accept payment in foreign currency.

A credit/debit card authorization form is a really simple one-page form you should generate and use for each client paying this way. It is a sound business practice. There are many examples available for free on the Internet that you can add your company name and logo to and use. The key take-away is to have something that lays out the client's name, the card information they will place on file, and gets them to sign consent for using the card. You also want to have a box they check that shows if the payment is a one-time charge or if they want to use it for recurring/additional payments should you go past the initial retainer deposit.

When it is time to charge the client again, they don't need to fill out a new credit/debit card authorization form out unless they are using a new card. Instead, simply have them write you a one sentence e-mail authorizing the additional payment. Some bank's credit cards may not recognize your company or put a fraud alert on the charge. They are simply protecting their customer as your retainer deposit will often be a large expense on their card. You can preempt this issue by telling the client to notify their bank that your company is an authorized provider of services.

I once had a woman call up asking why Lynx had not started work on her case. I was perplexed because I did not recognize her. I asked her to explain what she needed and who she had talked to. She explained what she needed and said she talked to a woman who collected her credit card payment over the phone. I was relieved because a woman could not have collected her credit card payment as I was the only person working at Lynx at the time, and the policy I still have to this day is to utilize the credit/debit card authorization form. Through additional questions, I determined she was not a scammer and had gone with a competitor in the area. I kindly directed her to them, so they could make good on what they charged her.

Invoicing

There are countless invoice software programs and templates out there to use for your business. You can use the payroll services mentioned earlier to handle invoices for you, or your CPA can do so if they offer bookkeeping. It is really up to you which to use. As you are working from a retainer, you'll list the cost of each service and subtract it against the money in the retainer account. The frequency of how often to provide an invoice is up to you. It will be based on the case you are working on and the case duration. Your due date should be upon the receipt regardless if it is in the middle of the investigation or at the conclusion of it. If you use an hourly or flat rate billing model, account for your time accurately on the invoice next to each service so the client knows exactly what they got.

If the work exceeds the amount in the retainer, immediately make contact with the client and rectify the situation. Lynx uses custom invoices from Invoicely that we make after the conclusion of each case. While they might take a little more time compared to an automated solution, I feel they look better than a generic one you would get from a software program.

Art of the Follow-Up

Sometimes the potential client needs time to think before they sign with you. There will be times they leave, hang up the phone, or are still on the fence. This is OK, you just have to learn to follow-up with them. This is a balance between trying to close the sale while simultaneously not coming off as needy. Some people will get distracted and forget to call you back. Some people don't have the authority to make a financial decision. Some people are standing on the edge and just need a little push to proceed.

I have learned the importance of finding the actual decision maker when dealing with corporate and individual clients alike. Sometimes, companies send someone out as a feeler searching for services. They are supposed to talk to you, then brief the person who has signature authority or control of the finances. This decision maker is the person you want to locate if you are wasting valuable time pitching to someone who can only facilitate a meeting with the person who can.

When dealing with couples who come to your office together, the same applies. One person usually is the final say on large cost items, you just to have to determine who it is. That is the person to whom you should direct your efforts. However, you probably won't know how much clout the other person exercises in the decision maker coming to a decision. Therefore, exercise caution with the other person and don't upset them by doing something rash like no longer talking to them or not making them feel valued.

If you have someone who is on the fence, schedule a follow-up with them during the initial contact. This way they are locked into re-contacting you. Give them some time to breathe, but not enough time to forget about the value or service you provide. A woman contacted Lynx regarding some surveillance where we would have to follow the ex-husband with the child to another state. She also wanted some social media investigation.

I did not initially close her during our telephonic consultation. When I called her back, I told her I was excited to start working on the case and that I had already peaked at his social media presence. I explained I had found some potentially good information, but I couldn't go any further since we weren't actually retained. She told me she was reluctant at the time because she didn't have the money, so she didn't know if it was a good idea to proceed forward. However, in light of this information, she would get her tax return upfront, that day, and provide it to us. She had to know, and it was enough to push her over the edge to retain us.

Try not to be too aggressive in following up with people. If they sense desperation, or being pushed around, they are not likely to retain you as it is off-putting. You are a professional and your time is valuable. They need you just as much as you need them. Try to personalize your follow-ups as much as possible and try to tie it to the value you are creating. Remind them how your service can help them get closure on their problem.

Many sales training programs teach the "three strikes and

you're out" concept. If you don't make contact with them on the third attempt or you can't close them by the third contact, then abort the mission. I once read it can take as many as nine contacts to close someone. This might work for selling vacuum cleaners door to door, but is entirely unnecessary for selling private investigation services. I do no more than three contacts with two follow-ups and include the original contact as the starting point.

Chapter 7
Running the Company

**"When you have exhausted all possibilities,
remember this. You haven't."
-Thomas Edison**

Running Things Smoothly

You have built the infrastructure, you have built out the back
end, and you have built out the front end. The doors are open.
But wait, there are some more things you need to know before
you break out the oversized novelty scissors and cut the welcome ribbon. Read on to find out.

Cloud Space

One of the core principles taught to Intelligence Officers,
military, and law enforcement personnel alike is the principle
of redundancy. One is none, two is one, three is better. Even if
your state requires hard copies of case files, you should maintain cloud storage for digitally uploading evidence, reports,
and anything else pertinent to your investigations. The cloud
is simply software and services that run across the Internet as
opposed to just on your computer hard drive. It helps your field

investigators with uploading large files while they are out and about. It helps you share large files with clients at the conclusion of their case.

There are multiple cloud space solutions available. The amount of data you can store is in the hundreds of terabytes or more and costs are getting cheaper by the day. These companies operate on a subscription platform and include all the large tech companies you already recognize such as Google and Amazon. These companies usually have enormous budgets in the hundreds of millions of dollars for cyber security, so your data is relatively protected. Lynx uses Amazon Web Services which runs the cloud for Amazon businesses. The options allow you to optimize your savings and storage size as your business grows.

Databases

One of the most important resources you have access to as a private investigation business owner are private databases that normal citizens can't access. Typically, only law enforcement has access to these databases. Remember, you are in the information business and need access to a robust number of databases. While the use of databases and the details behind open source intelligence searches far exceed the purpose of this book, you should know about the principle of redundancy.

Ideally, you will subscribe to at least three databases when you start off, and eventually to more. This kind of corroboration will aid you in the conduct of your investigations, as these databases are sometimes inaccurate or incomplete. For example, someone lives at Eastbrook Drive, but the clerk puts it in their file as East Brook or Eastbrooke Drive. When this data is packaged and sold to the database provider, its recorded erroneously like the above examples. You get what you pay for but remember you can always search free databases. You will be surprised with the results some free databases come up with. The fact that some of this information is available openly on these websites is downright scary. I would opt out of these sites yourself if you can while you are conducting a search.

Some private investigator databases are state specific such as Virginia's Extranet database to access Department of Motor Vehicle (DMV) records, or Atlas/RMV in Massachusetts to access driver records. Some private investigator databases require a commercial office and not a home office. Due to COVID-19, many companies who previously required this rule have relaxed it. Some will require an in-person inspection either by the company themselves or a third-party. They are looking for your ability to safeguard the information you will have access to. This goes for both the digital and physical space. Some place limitations on your access to information until you have a sustained relationship with them.

The fees vary widely to use these databases so take some time researching the public and private databases you plan to use. You can grant your employees user accounts and track their searches so you stay in regulatory compliance. Some databases truncate information which means they show you partial information, such as five of the nine digits of a SSN. You then pay a little more for the rest of the data if you need it. Remember, you are subject to an audit at any time, so accessing information on someone without a permissible purpose or having the signed services agreement to back you up could be a recipe for disaster. When Lynx first started off, we used the following paid databases:

• Tracers – Formerly Tracers Info. A sales representative told me Tracers was first started by a guy who wanted to help catch deadbeat dads. They allow you to have a home office as opposed to only a commercial office. There are few barriers to getting a Tracers account and they don't do a home inspection. I recommend you get a Tracers account as your first private database. You pay a monthly fee and for each search you conduct. Get started with them at https://www.tracers.com.

• Delvepoint – Delvepoint is a good compliment to Tracers. Like Tracers, you can have a home office. However, Delvepoint play the database truncation game meaning you need to hit Tracers or a related database first, then go back and run your checks with the information you have so you are not overpaying. Like Tracers, you pay a monthly fee and for each search you conduct. Get started with Delvepoint at https://www.delvepoint.com.

• TLO – a favorite of many private investigators and detectives in police departments. TLO is owned by Transunion, one of the big credit bureaus that have people's data. TLO allows you to have a home office but they will send someone to conduct an inspection. The commercial office inspection is a little more intense, but neither is insurmountable. Like Tracers and Delvepoint, you pay a monthly fee and for each search you conduct. Access TLO at https://www.tlo.com.

• CLEAR – CLEAR is popular in the federal government,

specifically federal law enforcement. Canadian conglomerate Thompson-Reuters owns them. Pre COVID-19, they did not allow you to have a home office. They are significantly more expensive monthly than the databases above, so it would be best to get them after you are established. You request a CLEAR account through https://legal.thomsonreuters.com and later access it through a different website.

- Skopenow – Skopenow is geared towards social media investigation and the insurance industry where it provides a scrape of all social media profiles of a subject. It is popular in the insurance fraud realm because Skopenow can pull photographs from social media to show physical activity which can help insurance investigators prove fraud. They have flexible payment options depending on the number of users and frequency of use. Check out Skopenow at https://www.skopenow.com.

- Datatree – This database was originally started to help realtors with property related information. However, they quickly found they could provide this information to private investigators. Lynx uses it for asset investigations. It is a great compliment to the open source public property records available. They have a subscription option and an option where you can pay a retainer up front, and each time you get a report the cost is pulled against the retainer. Get started with Datatree at https://www.datatree.com.

- PACER – Public Access to Court Electronic Records or PACER provides you access to court case information from federal appellate, district, and bankruptcy courts. The fee to pull a record is extremely nominal and is eliminated if you don't meet usage requirements for the quarter. Find PACER at https:// www.pacer.gov.

Lynx benefits greatly from having government-trained personnel do database style research so we don't always need the database information above. However, having immediate access to personally identifiable information on subjects and witnesses has proved invaluable time and time again. These can get you started, but don't forget to look into databases specific to your state or ones that will help on the dark web, dating websites, military records, etc. There are many other databases you can research and see if they are right for you. Some are free databases or free state specific databases. A mix of public and private databases will help paint a complete picture of the subject you are seeking.

Types of Reports

You have developed employee or independent contractor agreements. You have developed a services agreement. What about the actual deliverables you plan to give the client? Some private investigators don't want to produce a written report for fear of discovery. Others don't out of laziness. Even if your state does not require it, I recommend you provide a written product to your client unless they don't want one. People want something tangible that they can consume. It also adds a tinge of professionalism to your company. I have often been told both from the Intelligence Community and federal law enforcement that if it is not written down, it didn't happen. I consider report writing the most important of all private investigator skills. It may take time to write a report but once you develop your templates, it will get easier. Like the database section above, the actual writing of these reports far exceeds the purpose of this book. You should strive to break down your reports into the following categories:

• Investigative plan – an investigative plan is not actually a report, but it is still important. Once you are given the task of conducting an investigation, you should develop an investigative plan for the steps you will take. It should outline any special investigative techniques you might undertake to conduct the investigation. Your investigation will be much cleaner if you develop a plan for it.

• Surveillance report – you will use a surveillance report to document your physical surveillance activity of a subject or subjects of your investigation. You can embed pictures and links to videos of the activity you conducted. These should include a summary of the event, a detailed timeline, and any photos and video captured.

• Investigative report – this is a catch all report to document any investigative activity. You would also use it to record an interview of a subject or witness and detail what they said.

• Technical report – if you conducted a technical activity such as a camera installation, a GPS installation, computer forensics, etc., then you should write a technical report. It should explain the activity you undertook and how you did it.

• Closing report – called a Summary of Investigation or Report of Investigation in most law enforcement circles; this report should summarize the entirety of the investigation and list enclosures. The enclosures would be the additional reports that make up the case file. For example, a completed case file could have 10 surveillance reports, two investigative reports from interviews that took place, and the closing report.

You'll want to develop a records retention policy in accordance with your state laws. If you aren't sending these reports to the client electronically, send them with a quality paper that has some weight behind it as opposed to standard bulk copy paper. Something in the 24-32-pound range and made of a stronger material such as cotton. Until I started in entrepreneurship, I didn't realize paper was an art form. It is worth looking into choosing the right paper for the job. Your clients will notice.

Surveillance Policy

It is sound business practice to have your field investigators take some sort of arrival photo when they arrive at the surveillance scene. They should also take a no-activity shot approximately every 30 minutes when they are not on the move. When they close out the physical surveillance for the day, they should take a closing shot. These shots should be date/time stamped. Why do you do this? You do it for the field investigators out in the ether who like to operate in the gray. Some field investigators will say they went to a site when they didn't and magically couldn't locate the subject.

These investigators may leave a location early or leave to run an errand. These types of shots also help explain what you are doing to a client who does not understand surveillance. It sometimes involves hours of waiting around while you are billing them. If the client does not see any activity, they may think they are getting fleeced. Showing them those date/time stamped photos of periods of no activity helps prove otherwise.

You should have your field investigators keep a surveillance log of activity they witness. This is why I like Zellow, as it keeps date/time stamp recordings of the radio calls you made so the field investigators can go back later and fill out their reports with ease. When doing domestic investigation, your field investigators should treat the surveillance as an action sequence. They don't need to constantly be rolling the camera to get the moments that matter. This includes public displays of affection and activities that push the case over the preponderance of evidence threshold like walking into a hotel room. For insurance fraud cases, you want your field investigators to have constant roll. This is because you never know when a claimant will bend over, grab something, etc. when they are supposed to be incapacitated in some way. Basically, you don't know when they will conduct an activity that will compromise their claim. Of course, insurance companies love to have a pattern of behavior demonstrating their injury is not real.

Another sound business practice before your field investigators conduct physical surveillance is to provide a courtesy notification of surveillance to law enforcement in the area. This can be done via a call in, stopping by the police station in person, or by e-mail if the police department is set up that way. It is not required, but may alleviate their concerns when they receive calls about suspicious activity. This is inevitable if you do enough surveillance because some neighborhoods are difficult to set up in and some neighborhoods have legendary busybodies in them. You never know, the police might be nice and tell you some valuable intelligence about the neighborhood you are working in.

If you are writing it down in a memo format, your courtesy notification should be a simple one-page document. It should outline the vicinity of the area you are working in. It should not give all the information of the investigation just in case law enforcement or the clerk knows the person being surveilled. For example, you could say you are investigating insurance fraud case when its surveillance for an infidelity case.

If you have a pretext or ruse you are using, such as pretending to be a landscaping or contracting company, you can let the clerk or police officer know this. Hopefully, they will honor your request and tell any busybodies as much when they call in. Be advised, the clerk or police officer are under no obligation to do so. And if law enforcement asks for your credentials in the field, you need to cooperate and comply. If they are being professional, they will check your credentials and go about their business. You probably will have to relocate, but you can sometimes save yourself the trouble by sending your courtesy notification out.

Apps and Software

Technology is truly a godsend. There are so many apps and software out there to utilize to make your life easier. I can't keep up with all of them. I can only list the ones Lynx used when it was first formed and what it's currently using:

- Video editing – there are numerous platforms out there to edit your video clips. You can get insane with the number of tools and quality of content you want to produce. However, I don't think it is necessary to go with ultra-premium pro models like you are in Hollywood. Just make sure it has video editing necessities for investigation. One of those would be the ability to blur people's faces if your state and jurisdiction does not allow people to be in your video without their consent. Lynx uses Adobe Premiere Elements.

• Date/timestamps – Video Audio Timestamp Software or VATS is a powerful tool for adding date/time stamps to video and pictures your field investigators take during physical surveillance. You can also use it to strip audio from video when the jurisdiction you are recording in requires all parties consent to audio monitoring. Although the website seems sketchy based on its URL, it is legitimate, and you can get VATS from https://www.dts8888.com. It is also useful to get an application that can provide a GPS stamp if you are doing process serving like ServeManager. This provides irrefutable proof you visited a site location. The process serving field falls into the same issues as the private investigators I mentioned earlier.

• Surveillance communication – if you don't plan to use radios to conduct your team surveillance, then use the free Zellow app for your communication platform. You can put multiple users in a chat group, password protect it, and it runs off your cell signal. You can turn it into a walkie talkie concept by using the buttons of your cell phone. The range is the same as your cell phone, so you can talk over great distances which overcomes any line of site issues radios have. It records your radio calls and date/time stamps them so you can go back later and cross reference your calls for your surveillance report. You can download Zellow in either the Android Store or the Apple Store.

• Travel – your time is valuable. You want to minimize your time on the road if possible. The RoadWarrior app minimizes travel time by picking the best route between multiple stops. Not only is this good for private investigation when you have multiple interviews, you can also use it for service of process assignments in order for your field investigators to hit multiple stops in a timely manner.

• Security – you need to protect and privatize your searching of websites. Enter Virtual Private Networks (VPN). You can use VPNs as an app on your phone or software on your computer. Any solid version will do such as TunnelBear or Rocket. There are free and paid versions available. Privacy does not equal anonymity and vice versa when you use a VPN. Lynx uses the Proton VPN.

Task Tracking & Scheduling

Once operations are up and running, you need to keep track of all the tasks going on in the company including everything you and your employees need to do. Deadlines keep you on track. There are many solutions out there dedicated to providing task tracking service. Lynx uses Asana. Asana is free to get started with and is relatively inexpensive once you start to grow. You can create projects a.k.a. investigations, checklists with tasks, assign team members to work on them, and set deadlines. You can communicate through the platform as well. Asana is a versatile solution that works for any company setup.

Once you manage more than one investigation, you will need to coordinate assigning case managers and field investigators to the case. You also will need a solution to track your workers' time spent on a case and their location when involved on a case. This is where TSheets comes in. TSheets is a time tracking software that can greatly minimize your time spent managing an investigation. TSheets also generates a log of how many hours a worker worked on a case which can help with payroll and for invoicing. It scales with you as your staff grows. TSheets has been of great benefit to Lynx for these reasons. You can get started with TSheets at (*) www.tsheets.com/#a:lynx-securitygroup

Investigator Location

Lynx uses a variety of independent contractors to supplement case load when there is an influx of work. When I first started out, I would send a "mass e-mail blast" out to all independent contractors to see who wanted to work on the case. If you do this, make sure you do it as a blind CC or BCC to protect your independent contractors' privacy. I later decided it would be easier to target the case requests based on who had the skills to do so and their location. I created a map on Google maps with all known independent contractors that worked for Lynx.

It includes the investigator's name, phone number, e-mail address, any special skills, and their home of record. This way, with one quick look, I can swiftly identify who can back us up on a case Lynx just took on. To create one of these maps, simply go to Google and search Google Maps. Then start labeling your personnel.

Using Linguists

I have no facility with languages so it is much easier to hire out assistance with translation than learn the foreign languages in the areas Lynx operates in. I have benefited from contacts at graduate school and in government who speak a variety of foreign languages. I can rely on these people to help me. This is not the case for everyone. If you work in a diverse area, I recommend ensuring you have the ability to retain a client that does not speak English. Far too often, Lynx has had people call or e-mail who speak no English or very limited English.

It might be easy to find to someone who speaks a language like Spanish, but what about something like Korean? A lady e-mailed Lynx asking us in one broken English sentence to have a Korean speaking investigator call her back. That was the extent of the message. Luckily, we have someone who speaks the language, but it could have easily been something else we were not prepared for.

You can hire bilingual field investigators to help you. You can also utilize a linguist service on a contractual basis and bring them in when necessary. It is more difficult to get a linguist to translate on the phone during a conference call as opposed to right next to you. It is much easier to pay extra and have the linguist appear in person.

I have worked with dozens of linguists worldwide on multiple continents, but not everyone has had that luxury. Working with linguists can be an art form. You need to establish a policy and provide training for your workers who have never worked with a linguist. For example, ensure your investigators and case managers actually direct conversation towards the client, witness, or subject as opposed to talking to the linguist to help build rapport.

There are two generally accepted forms of translation and that is the alternating method and simultaneous method. The alternating method is far more common and involves you speaking, the linguist translating, the other person responding, then the linguist translating that information back to you. The simultaneous method involves the linguist translating as you speak and involves a much higher level of skill and education level. The alternating translation is often easier on everyone.

Since your linguist will be privy to confidential information a client will wish to keep private, make sure they sign your independent contractor agreement with a non-disclosure clause in it. Establishing a linguist policy now will help you attract non-English speaking clients and set you up to work internationally.

Hierarchy

There is no one way to structure your chain of command or hierarchy of your workers. You need to have a management workflow without so many layers of management it turns into a government bureaucracy. Private investigation companies can be very different. One acceptable method is to have the bottom layer as field investigators who report to case managers who report to company leadership. You also have your support staff such as receptionists and linguists who report directly to company leadership. Some of the roles break down as follows:

• Field investigators – these personnel conduct investigative activity. They pull records, conduct physical surveillance, conduct investigative interviews, write reports, and do the full gamut of investigative field work.

• Case managers – field investigators report to case managers who provide oversight of their case, develop the investigative plan for the field investigators, serve as surveillance controllers, proofread reports, and provide additional support to field investigators if needed. It is best to use case managers who first served as a field investigator so they know what the duties entail and can actually use their experience to help the field investigator.

• Support staff – an overarching term to encompass all the other people in your company that don't have an investigative role but make your company work such as receptionists, linguists, mechanics, sales representatives, bookkeepers, etc. They should report to company leadership.

• Company leadership – made up of you and any other managing members or corporate officers who oversee all company operations.

There is no one accepted way to structure your personnel. When I first started Lynx, it was just me so I did all the support duties and investigative activity myself. This quickly became impossible, so I brought on independent contractors to lighten the load before I brought on my first part-time employee. I prefer independent contractors to employees and have streamlined the process using them. This is due to the large number of professionals in my network. If you don't have a large professional network to draw from yet, you might want to go the traditional employee route starting with part-time employees before converting them to full-time employees. Regardless of the route you choose, building a structure your workers can understand will increase workplace efficiency and make it easier for your company to scale.

Building Business Credit

When your business is first established, it will have no credit. It will be incumbent upon you as the owner to build its credit. If you want to scale, you will need business credit. Building business credit will separate your personal interests from your business interests. Businesses have credit reports just like people do. The bureaus that provide business credit reports are Dun & Bradstreet, Experian, and Equifax.

I recommend you get a business credit card and start opening trade lines with different vendors that report to the business credit bureaus. Once you hit the black as opposed to the red, you will also start getting offers in the mail for business lines of credit to help you grow. Just like your personal credit, pay your bills on time or early. When the vendors get paid, they will start offering you those favorable net terms I mentioned earlier in the Equipment List section which will also help build your business credit. You can then use your business credit to negotiate lower insurance rates, lease or buy property, get a line of credit to purchase equipment, and initially pay salaries when you take on a staff.

Limited Reciprocity Agreements

Eventually, you will have an investigation that forces your company to cross state lines to continue the investigation. If you initiate an investigation in your home state and need to cross state lines, it is OK to do so for a period, usually between 15 and 30 days. Of course, this depends on your state laws and the laws of the state the investigation is taking you into.

Louisiana, Virginia, North Carolina, Oklahoma, Florida, Tennessee, and Georgia all have limited reciprocity agreements with other states. Laws change constantly, so you have to stay on top of this. You should not solicit new business out of state or ever try to initiate a case out of state. I always check with Lynx's counsel before running a case that will take us out of state.

Chapter 8
Things I Wish I Knew

"In school, you're taught a lesson and then given a test. In life, you're given a test that teaches you a lesson."
-Tom Bodett

Catch-All

This chapter is more of a catch-all than anything else. It includes some of my experiences and insights while navigating the private investigation realm.

Physical Image

If someone tells you physical image doesn't matter as a private investigation business owner, they are lying to you. However, it certainly is not the be all and end all. Taking care of yourself is important. People unfortunately associate physical image with competence and likeability. Little things you can do are to control your body weight and minimize the number of visible tattoos—this is where a suit can help. Tattoos are becoming more accepted in society but it is still the equivalent of an albatross around your neck in certain professional circles so tread lightly.

The Power of the Suit

I usually wear a two-piece suit when I am doing sales for the company and meeting with potential clients. The other times I wear khakis with a Lynx branded polo. Why? It lends itself to the concept of the power of legitimacy. For some reason, people equate the suit with authority. I have actually lost count of how many private investigation business owners don't do this. I know one investigator who runs a small show and goes to work in sweatpants! How could someone take you seriously? I remember reading a *Reader's Digest* article where the brother of a woman with a complicated pregnancy said he would be there at the hospital dressed in a three-piece suit during delivery. When she asked him why, he told her, "If something goes wrong, and I am in a three-piece suit, people will listen to me." In my opinion, nothing has changed.

I once had a client who wouldn't make eye contact with me. She then blurted out she was very intimidated by me because of my suit! I spoke to another client with another investigator wearing jeans and a polo. When I walked in, the client said, "Are you an attorney?" Another client came to me and when I was gathering the information for the case, she exclaimed, "You are so much more professional than the first guy I talked to. He looked like he lived in a homeless shelter." What you wear could tip the client into signing on the dotted line in your favor. The suit doesn't have to be Brioni, but it does have to be tailored. I recommend having a few different base colors such a black, gray, and navy. From here, you can experiment with different dress shirt colors, patterns, and ties.

GPS Tracking Devices

You have to be careful with GPS tracking laws as they vary from state to state for the private sector. As a sound business practice, you might want to take the stance of California and only agree to affix them in or to a vehicle if there is consent. Basically, California Penal Code – PEN § 637.7 states if the registered owner, lessor, or lessee of a vehicle has consented to the use of the electronic tracking device with respect to that vehicle, it is OK to use one on the vehicle. The consent applies if you place it under the car, in the car, or hard wire it into the vehicle itself. The GPS installation is easy to do in a domestic investigation when the husband and wife are on the same vehicle registration and one is hiring you to surveil the other. But what if it is a girlfriend/boyfriend situation or an employee/employer situation? Again, check your state laws and speak to your attorney because you don't want to get involved in stalking. Some states have not yet clearly defined a precedent for GPS law, so there is a lot of gray area for an investigator to work with.

If a client wants you to use a GPS device, it might make sense from a business stance for them to purchase it or rent it from you. This is because there is a chance the device might be discovered and subsequently removed or confiscated. You don't want to be out several hundred dollars if this happens. While the device is considered a capital expense for the business, it is still better to prepare for this potential issue and charge accordingly. Lynx charges for the install, de-install, and monitoring of the device, but we also almost always go for the "deep" installation to minimize compromise. As in, there is little chance of detection unless you are specifically looking through the internal vehicle wiring components or internal vehicle components to find something. Close to 99.9 percent of people do not do this when they turn on their car. You can't do this without legal access to the vehicle.

Private Investigator Law

Learning about the law when you are going through a local, state, or federal law enforcement training academy is easy. It is built into the curriculum. It is not always so easy when you are in private investigation and no one tells you anything. This is most true in states with little to no training or licensing requirements. Sure, some states do build it into mandated training, but most do not. When I first started in private investigation, I simply read as much as I could about laws pertaining to private investigation. Look at the genesis of most private investigation law. It usually comes from someone doing something stupid in the field and everyone else paying for that incompetence.

For example, in 1989, Robert Bardo, a man suffering from mental illness, shot and killed actress Rebecca Schaeffer. Bardo had gotten Schaeffer's address from a private investigator that retrieved the information from the California DMV. These actions along with some others paved the way for the creation of the Driver's Privacy Protection Act of 1994 which protects address information that DMVs have. You can only get this information from the DMV today with a permissible purpose. Private investigation is one of those purposes, but states have the authority to make their own stricter laws. Some states still do not provide information to third-party databases that private investigators use. Others give it up like a drunk girl on prom night. The databases you subscribe to will let you know what information is available and what is not.

At the very least, the federal laws I would look into include the Driver's Privacy Protection Act of 1994, Fair Credit Reporting Act of 1970, Gramm–Leach–Bliley Act of 1999, Fair Debt Collection Practices Act of 1977, Electronic Communications Privacy Act of 1986, Digital Millennium Copyright Act of 1998, and Katz v. United States, 389 U.S. 347 (1967). For your state, I would look into audio monitoring consent laws (one party consent vs. all party consent), GPS laws, and any laws governing the conduct of private investigation.

If you use full credit report information, it is considered a sound business practice to set up a separate company to pull full credit reports for tenant screenings and pre-employment background investigation/checks. Tenant screenings are used by landlords to evaluate prospective tenants to determine if they will meet their obligation to pay rent and not damage your property. Some databases such as Tracers requires a five-year relationship with them before they give you full credit report information. One party consent vs. all party consent for audio recording is very important. If you live in a state that requires all party consent, you must strip the audio away from any video your capture. This is easily done with software like VATS. Laws constantly change and you should stay up to date with them.

Dealing with Difficult Clients

When I first started out, a woman called Lynx and said she was burglarized. She said that the police did nothing, and she wanted justice. She wanted to know who the perpetrator or perpetrators were and for them to be prosecuted to the fullest extent of the law. She demanded to know what Lynx would do differently from the police. I explained to her where private investigation could pick up where law enforcement left off. I explained how we would go about the case and that we would leave no stone unturned. Not only did she sharp shoot me with statements like, "Yeah, you would leave no stone unturned as long as the money doesn't run out" but she also said, "How do I know you weren't in on the burglary?" What would you say to someone saying things like this? Is this someone you want to work for?

Some potential clients you work with are used to throwing their money around to get what they want. Remember, you are under no obligation to take their case. When you encounter people like this, you can simply tell them you can't assist them. The money is not worth it. You could refer them to another investigations company. These are the kind of people who give you a 3:00 AM phone call or threaten to sue you when they perceive a slight (real or imagined).

Firearms

I am a strong supporter of firearms and the right to carry, but I don't allow independent contractors to carry when they are doing work for Lynx. Why? Normally employers are not vicariously liable for acts independent contractors commit unless the work is considered an inherently dangerous activity. Basically, if there is an increased chance of injury, your company can be found liable. They don't have to work for Lynx if they don't like the policy. Since most enjoy getting paid two to three times the average pay rate of a comparable investigator, or what they normally would get, we get a high compliance rate.

Remember, insurance rates will also go up drastically when you bring firearms into the mix. Consider a firearms policy for your employees in your employee handbook, especially if you plan to have them do interviews and physical surveillance in bad neighborhoods.

Using Family Members to Work in Your Business

When I first started out, I had experienced some hubris and thought bringing on a family member would save on expenses despite warnings not to do so. He signed on as an independent contractor. I involved him in matters I normally would have not involved other employees or independent contractors. One day, we landed a $20,000 retainer and I CC'ed him on the correspondence. Naturally, he expected 50 percent of this, but I was paying all the overhead costs, I held all the liability as the business owner, and did all the work to find, recruit, and land this client. I put together the proposal, assembled the team and equipment, and developed the schedule for this particular case among other things. It didn't matter, he still expected 50 percent of the gross retainer. Of course, this led to a division amongst us and him parting ways with the company. Family is good for everything except working in your business. If you use family, I urge you to be cognizant of my story.

Family Members as Clients

At a party, I spoke to a family member about work and my private investigation business came up. She was elated the business was going well and asked me to help a friend of hers out, at family price. If you don't know what family price is yet, it is a synonym for free. Running a business is not free though and a mantra that has developed is you are running a business not a charity. I declined, especially when she told me what the woman had in mind. Now, you do have the flexibility as a business owner to do something pro bono, it is even a good way to get publicity, but you should not feel coerced by a family member. Sometimes it's best to politely decline and avoid the headache.

Reinvesting Profits

When you first consistently stay in the black and are out of the red, it can be tempting to look at the profit in the business account as yours. Well, it is, but don't be so quick to spend everything on yourself. You should be setting money aside towards growing the business. This reinvesting strategy will pay dividends in its own right as you scale. Some ideas:

- Advertising – it never hurts to expand your advertising and marketing budget to exponentially grow your client base.

- Capital expenses – if there is new equipment you were eying for the business, you should purchase it.

- Cash emergency fund – having a cash emergency fund is essential to weather future financial storms. Look at COVID-19. No one saw a pandemic coming, and many businesses didn't have cash reserves for six months, let alone one month. Always set money aside for the unexpected.

- Continuing education – invest in yourself and your employees' training and education.

- Talent management – bring on new employees and do so at a higher salary rate than competitors provide so they stick around.

Safety Net

I mentioned a safety net in the preface of this book. What I mean is an actual job. Some people think the cold turkey do or die approach is the best method for starting a business. Meaning, you cut ties with everything and jump headfirst into starting and growing your business. I feel it is OK to still have a job still while you start building your business. When you consistently stay in the black, you can then cut ties with it and go full time. Most law enforcement, military, and government personnel wait until their pension has kicked in before starting their company. This in itself is a form of safety net. Again, be cognizant of state laws because some states like New Jersey do not allow people actively engaged in law enforcement to hold private investigator credentials for conflict of interest fears. This is all just some food for thought when you are thinking about starting your business.

Generalist vs. Specialist

Science-fiction author Robert Heinlein said, "A human being should be able to change a diaper, plan an invasion, butcher a hog, conn a ship, design a building, write a sonnet, balance accounts, build a wall, set a bone, comfort the dying, take orders, give orders, cooperate, act alone, solve equations, analyze a new problem, pitch manure, program a computer, cook a tasty meal, fight efficiently, die gallantly. Specialization is for insects." It might be a hard pill to swallow for those who currently specialize, but if you run a business, you need to be a generalist. It took me awhile to learn that it is the generalists that oversee the specialists in a business. Specialists are extremely important to the success of your business, but you have to wear your generalist hat as you direct all the operations and facets of your business. You need to have a base understanding of what your specialists do, but also see the big picture to manage the whole company.

There is a famous saying floating around the ether attributed to many people such as Albert Einstein that says you don't have to know everything, you just have to know where to find it. For example, Lynx offers computer forensics. I currently have a rudimentary understanding of the process. I possess enough knowledge to brief it, but not enough to go into the weeds for it. That is why I have a specialist who works for me and can go into the weeds if necessary, should the client require it. I know where to find the answer if I need to. It comes back to talent management and allocation of your time and resources.

Forward Momentum and Leadership

I mentioned the skill of human capital earlier. There is another concept known as forward momentum which you might want to employ when you first start out. Forward momentum is always propelling the business forward because you have multiple skills to do so. For example, one day you do some surveillance, the next day you do a polygraph examination, the next day you do a K-9 search of a high school where drugs are suspected of being stashed.

You can only do this once you possess multiple skills that you have either gained through experience or continuing education. It keeps you from being stagnant and prevents you from being stuck getting an income stream from only one service provided. Be careful not to take on too many new skills at once or that will defeat the purpose of forward momentum. Focus on building one service up until it is running the way you want it to, then add a new service using the concept. You will amplify this skill with your employees and independent contractors who will do the work for you. It will become part of your management style which should include management by walking around.

Management by walking around is something I learned from Aristotle and Daniel Schwartz. Aristotle once said, "He who cannot be a good follower cannot be a good leader." Meaning, it's key you understand a skill at the lowest level before you move into the management of it. Daniel Schwartz is now the executive chairman of Restaurant Brands International which is the parent company to restaurants like Burger King and

Popeyes. When Schwartz assumed the role as CEO of Burger King at 32 years old, he had no restaurant management experience so he started from the ground up in Burger King. He worked the drive thru, he made burgers, and he scrubbed toilets. He went on to corporate middle management to examine those processes and saw where there was bloating and where he could make cuts.

The lesson here is if you want to add a service to your business, you might want to engage in it yourself so you know how it will work for your company. When I first started, I only had my Intelligence Community and military experience to draw from. I had never done things like service of process and private sector executive protection. So, I started from the ground up. For example, I did process serves for $15 to understand the field before I offered the service for my own company and had others do it for me.

Badges and Citizen's Arrest

Depending on your state law, you may be authorized to carry a badge instead of just a credential card. I don't carry a private investigator badge even though I am authorized to do so in my state. The lines can get easily blurred with people thinking you are law enforcement. It is much easier to just carry your credential card. There have been private investigators who get tripped up by trying to impersonate law enforcement or at least make it look like they are without saying so. You can do the same thing with your credential card as with a badge. If you want to use a private investigator badge for your employees, ensure you have the use and misuse of it written into your employee handbook so there is no ambiguity, especially when someone is representing your company.

A citizen's arrest is the ability for a non-sworn law enforcement officer, a private citizen, to arrest someone for a crime committed. Making a citizen's arrest, if allowed in your state, has virtually a 100 percent downside and no upside. With potential liability issues and criminal charges such as kidnapping, wrongful arrest, false imprisonment, and unlawful restraint, there is no reason you want your business entangled in this. Lynx doesn't allow its workers to make a citizen's arrest. Again, it is so easy to get the lines blurred. At least law enforcement officers have a vast overarching protection called qualified immunity that private investigators don't which provides them with a special legal shield from certain liability. Lay out the provisions within your employee handbook so your investigators know exactly what their limits are.

Chapter 9
Conclusion

**"Two roads diverged in a wood and I –
I took the one less traveled by, and that
has made all the difference."
-Robert Frost**

Your Competition

Don't be so arrogant to think that you know everything and get comfortable where you are at. There is someone out there who is hungry and will get your potential clients if you allow it. You must study your competition. Take their courses, understand their products, read the reviews, subscribe to their e-mail list, watch what they do. Then do it better. This is the only way to succeed. Remember, struggle is part of the human condition.

Organizations to Join

The work you will put into your private investigation business will never cease. Even when you are away from the office or on vacation, you will be thinking about it. It is your baby and you want to see it thrive. One way to help get your name out there is to network and meet potential clients by joining certain organizations in your community and in your work sphere. You need to be picky about this. Some will require substantial time commitments. Others are not worth the membership fee whether it's through poor management, or misuse of your time. Here are some I have found credible:

•   ASIS International – ASIS International was founded in 1955 with a focus on security management. As I mentioned before in the Private Investigation Defined section, it is the closest thing private investigation has to board certification and that comes from the international recognition of ASIS in the security and investigations field along with their certifications. ASIS has chapters across the U.S. and in many countries, which can lead to great networking opportunities. You will have to pay membership dues to be a part of this organization. Get started with ASIS International at https://www.asisonline.org.

•   Association of Certified Fraud Examiners (ACFE) – ACFE is a highly respected organization founded in 1988 with an emphasis on fraud. Not only is it made up of those who investigate fraud, it has accountants and attorneys amongst its membership rolls. Like ASIS International, ACFE has chapters around the world that offer excellent networking opportunities. You can pay membership dues and can get started with ACFE by visiting https://www.acfe.com.

•   National Association of Legal Investigators (NALI) – NALI was founded in 1967 to bridge the gap in the legal investigation field as there was no certifying body for this niche field. The primary goal of the organization is to enhance the growth of the legal investigation field. Find out more by visiting https://www.nalionline.org.

• The Public Record Retriever Network (PRRN) – get listed as a company who is willing and able to pull public records from government establishments such as courthouses and bureaus of vital records. These will most likely be court and county records. Not all records are online so you might need someone to do a local pull for you to further your investigation. They also cover some other countries as well. You can join PRRN online at http://www.prrn.us.

• World Association of Detectives (WAD) – WAD was founded in 1925 and serves as another association of professionals in the field of private investigation. It is a useful starting point to locate international investigators you will need to assist with international investigations. Likewise, people can find you using the same methods, regardless if they are a member or not. Just like ASIS International and ACFE, you'll owe membership dues and can get started with WAD at https://www.wad.net.

There are also state specific organizations such as the California Association of Licensed Investigators or the Private Investigation Association of Virginia. Just like the national and international organizations above, you should determine if it is worth your time to join them. PInow (http://www.pinow.com) maintains a great list of state private investigation associations. There are also niche investigation organizations such as the National Association of Fire Investigators. Simply run an Internet search to determine if there is an organization that fits with your niche of investigation.

Continuing Education, Training, and Certifications

Learning is a lifelong process. It is even more important when you are an entrepreneur. You should become a voracious reader of anything related to business and private investigation. You should attend as many training courses as possible to develop skills, both hard and soft, that will further the growth of your business. For inspiration, watch the 2011 documentary Jiro Dreams of Sushi. It follows legendary sushi chef Jiro Ono and his strive for perfection consistent with Japanese culture. Ono is considered a shokunin in Japan, meaning artisan or craftsman. But it is much more than this. Being a shokunin is actually considered a way of life, an honor you bestow upon someone in their chosen profession. This is the kind of attitude you should put towards your private investigation business.

Not everyone has the luxury of being government trained and there are many excellent private sector programs available. Here are some skills you and your employees should build or maintain for your wheelhouses:

• Report writing – any course taken at a college can help make you a better writer. Alternatively, you can use paid and free online courses from learning platforms such as Coursera (https://www.coursera.org) and Udemy (https://www.udemy.com). When I was a kid, you could not pay me to read a book or write something. Now, I not only read dozens of books a year, I wrote a book! Never underestimate how important this skill is. I try to get better with my writing every day.

- Open Source Intelligence (OSINT) – you and your workers need training on the latest and greatest open source intelligence and database search techniques. Michael Bazzell has an excellent OSINT course you can take online or through live training. You can find his course at https://www.inteltechniques.com.

- Investigative interviewing – another skill that serves as a foundation to your business. There are several reputable training courses out there that will teach you their system of interviewing and interrogation. These include The Reid Technique from John E. Reid & Associates, Inc. at https://www.reid.com, Practical Kinesics Interview and Interrogation Course from Stan B. Walters & Associates, Inc. at https://www.thelieguy.com, Scientific Content Analysis or SCAN from Laboratory of Scientific Interrogation, Inc. at https://www.lsiscan.com, and Interview and Interrogation Techniques from Wicklander-Zulawski & Associates, Inc at https://www.w-z.com.

- Physical surveillance – another foundational skill for your business. Even if you have received on-the-job training from another job or from the government, it never hurts to learn new techniques. There are multiple online-only surveillance courses. These are good for learning tips and tricks, but you absolutely need to get out on the ground to practice this skill with live training. Unfortunately, I have not come across a U.S. based live course I can recommend for private investigators other than Lynx's at this time. The rest are geared for military, law enforcement, and intelligence students only. If you look internationally, you can go with ISS Training Limited in the United Kingdom. Find more information at https://www.

intelsecurity.co.uk.

• Public speaking – this skill will be helpful when you present your service at a conference or other event. It also will come in handy if you decide to venture off into training. Many people are downright afraid to present to a live audience. There are courses you can take online and in-person to assist you. Toastmasters International, founded in 1924, can be a great club to join to help you with public speaking. Visit https://www. toastmasters.org for more information.

• Negotiation – negotiation training will help you and your client reach a "win win" scenario, especially a corporate investigation client. You can attend negotiations training courses throughout the U.S. and you can get them at business schools. The first negotiation course I took was through Karrass Limited. Find out more at https://www.karrass.com.

• Sales – sales are the lifeblood to running your private investigation business. Like negotiations training, you can attend sales training programs through business schools or other stand-alone courses through the U.S. Sales and negotiations training often go hand in hand.

• Drones – if you want to add aerial surveillance to your field investigators' toolkits, consider drone training and certification. You or they will have to pass the Part 107 Federal Aviation Administration testing in order to get your drone license for commercial purposes. There are now several online and several in-person schools available for you to pursue this avenue.

• TSCM – If you plan to offer TSCM services, and you or

your techs did not get trained at ITC, you will have to pursue private sector training. Research Electronics International (REI) offers the best private sector equivalent training courses compared to ITC's suite of courses. Find out more about training through REI by visiting https://www.reiusa.net.

- Photography – photography is often overlooked during surveillance training courses, but knowing how to utilize audio, video, and camera equipment will help present a professional product for your clients. You can take photography courses throughout the U.S. at colleges and private schools. For surveillance photography courses specifically, you run into the same problems that you run into with physical surveillance training courses, and that is courses only geared towards military, law enforcement, and intelligence entities. You can look internationally again to ISS Training Limited for surveillance photography training.

Depending on your state, you may be required to complete continuing education annually to maintain compliance for your individual and business license. It is incumbent upon you to maintain this compliance as the government organizations responsible for licensing do not have any obligation to notify you. Your continuing education could be something as simple as eight hours of training for the year. You should be striving to far exceed this standard by attending courses like the ones mentioned above. The Lynx Criminal Justice Academy is a place you can train on many of these skills and more. You can do so through a mixture of online and live training courses. Contact us if you would like a complete tailored training solution for your employees so you can minimize overhead and bring on trained employees ready to work.

There are countless certifications out there. Just like the organizations you are considering joining, some are not worth anything while others add that additional legitimacy you need to close the sale while demonstrating your knowledge. The following certifications are geared towards the various fields of private investigation and can give you and your employees something to strive for:

• Professional Certified Investigator or PCI – ASIS International offers this credential. The PCI provides independent verification of your skills as an investigator.

• Certified Fraud Examiner or CFE – ACFE offers this credential. It demonstrates your knowledge of fraud detection and prevention.

• Certified Legal Investigator or CLI – NALI offers this credential. It attests to your competence in the skills necessary to assist an attorney with litigation preparation through your investigation work. Find out more about the CLI and NALI from https://www.nalionline.org.

• Certified Reid Technique or CRT – This credential is held by John E. Reid & Associates, Inc. It shows your knowledge and skill in using the Reid Technique for interviewing and interrogation.

• Certified Forensic Interviewer or CFI – The International Association of Interviewers (IAI) maintains this credential. It serves as a display of your overall skills in interview and interrogation. Learn more at https://www.certifiedinterviewer. com.

- Certified Fire and Explosion Investigator or CFEI – if you plan to work in private investigation with an emphasis on arson and explosion investigations, you can look into the CFEI. The credential is controlled under the auspices of the National Association of Fire Investigators (NAFI) who were founded in 1961. Find out more about the CFEI and NAFI at https://www.nafi.org.

Interconnected Fields

As your business grows, you may wish to provide other services. You will quickly realize that the skills you utilize in private investigation are linked to other career fields such as security guard work, bail enforcement, executive protection, repossession, training, and process serving. You can even look into becoming an expert witness. Many private investigation companies offer these services in addition to their standard investigation skills. Just like private investigation, it varies from state to state if you are allowed to market services in these related fields or if you need a separate license to do so. Some states like Virginia highly regulate each field. Others like California enable you to do things like executive protection with a private investigation license. Once you build out your private investigation practice, I encourage you to carry your skills over into these interconnected fields. It plays into the forward momentum concept and forces you to continue innovating and learning.

Chapter 10
Resources

"Only the educated are free."
-Epictetus

Resources to Aid You

To make things easy for you, I will lay out some additional resources to help you start your private investigation business. I have provided you a layout of virtually all the aspects you need to complete in order to get your private investigation business started. Here are some books I recommend:

- *Accounting for Dummies: 6th Edition* by John A. Tracy

- *Art of the Start 2.0: The Time-Tested, Battle-Hardened Guide for Anyone Starting Anything* by Guy Kawasaki

- *How to Open & Operate a Financially Successful Private Investigation Business: With Companion CD-ROM* by Michael Cavallaro

- *How to Win Friends & Influence People* by Dale Carnegie

- *Influence: The Psychology of Persuasion* by Robert B. Cialdini

- *Introduction to Conducting Private Investigations: Private Investigator Entry Level (02E)* by Philip A. Becnel IV

- *Million Dollar Consulting: The Professional's Guide to Growing a Practice, Fifth Edition* by Alan Weiss

- *Never Split the Difference: Negotiating as if Your Life Depended on It* by Chris Voss

- *Rich Dad Poor Dad: What the Rich Teach Their Kids About Money That the Poor and Middle Class Do Not!* by Robert T. Kiyosaki

- *Run Your Own Corporation: How to Legally Operate and Properly Maintain Your Company Into the Future* by Garrett Sutton

- *Start Your Own Corporation: Why the Rich Own Their Own Companies and Everyone Else Works for Them* by Garrett Sutton

- *Tax-Free Wealth: How to Build Massive Wealth by Permanently Lowering Your Taxes* by Tom Wheelwright

- *The Complete Idiot's Guide to Private Investigating, Third Edition: Discover How the Pros Uncover the Facts and Get to the Truth* by Steven Kerry Brown

- *The Everything Private Investigation Book: Master the Techniques of the Pros to Examine Evidence, Trace Down People, and Discover the Truth* by Sheila L. Stephens

- *The E-Myth Revisited: Why Most Small Businesses Don't Work and What to Do About It* by Michael E. Gerber

- *The Mission, the Men, and Me: Lessons from a Former Delta Force Commander* by Pete Blaber

- *Think and Grow Rich* by Napoleon Hill
- *Value-Based Fees: How to Charge – and Get – What You're Worth* by Alan Weiss

Aside from the resources above, look forward to many more books from me to aid you on your journey!

Action Time

You have completed *How to State a Private Investigation Business: A Proven Blueprint for Success.* You only have one thing left to do—take action! Think about the trials and tribulations being an entrepreneur can bring to you. Think about how you can help your fellow man while becoming wealthy. Remember, an idea is nothing. The execution of the idea is everything. I wish you the best of luck in your future endeavors.

If I Can Help You Further

If you would like personal attention to start or grow your private investigation business, please e-mail me at edward@lynxsecuritygroup.com so we can promptly connect.

Thank You

Thank you for reading *How to Start a Private Investigation Business: A Proven Blueprint for Success.* I hope you can see how to start your private investigation business and will take the appropriate actions to do so. The U.S. needs entrepreneurs to spearhead the growth of the economy. If I helped you, please consider leaving a review for this book wherever you purchased it from.

Acknowledgements

As I mentioned in the book, when I was younger, you could not pay me to read a book let alone write something. I could not have imagined in my wildest dreams actually writing a book and self-publishing it. As I have gotten older, I learned to conceptualize an idea and then attack it. However, with this idea, I could not have gotten to the finish line without some others along the way. I need to thank the following people in no particular order:

To my editor Joanne Lane for catching my numerous writing mistakes and reminding me that only the U.S. Military writes in such a quasi-version of the English language that it might as well be a language from outer space.

To my book designer and typesetter Molly Brooks for creating the book cover for this book and for turning my manuscript into a real book through her typesetting ability.

To my sister Mary Panico for marketing this book and getting it out to all the people who wish to learn how to build and run a private investigation company.

To the clients of Lynx who took a chance on my company. Thank you for entrusting us with your investigation and helping this company grow.

To the employees, independent contractors, and team of advisors for Lynx. You are the ones who made it all possible with your contributions to the cause.

To my brother Dominic Panico and my cousin Armando Palmieri for reading through the earlier drafts of this book and ensuring I provided as much helpful content as I could.

To my amazing wife Angela. Who constantly puts up with the early mornings, late nights, and countless hours of domestic and international travel for work. Whose patience with my ideas and ability to pull me back down to reality for the crazy ones is second to none. Who is my most trusted advisor and best friend. And of course, who deserves a medal for putting up with my constant changes to this book as she was the sounding board for it. I love you.

About the Author

Edward Panico is the founder of Lynx Security Group, a private investigation, security consulting, and training company. He has spent considerable time teaching private investigators of all experience levels. Mr. Panico has created a wide variety of private investigation classes including classroom based and field-based training. Mr. Panico has assisted other private investigator entrepreneurs with opening and expanding their investigations companies. He has also mentored aspiring private investigators on everything from which career path they should choose to assisting with out-of-state job placement.

For over 16 years, Mr. Panico has worked both domestically and abroad in intelligence, investigations, and security matters with the U.S. Military and with the U.S. Department of State. Mr. Panico has trained hundreds of domestic and foreign military, intelligence, and private sector personnel across the globe in security and counterintelligence. While employed with the U.S. Military and U.S. Department of State, he received extensive training and experience in risk mitigation, anti-terrorism/force protection, crime prevention, criminal investigation, counterintelligence, dignitary protection, physical security, access control, security operations, intelligence collection, investigations, interview/interrogations, and physical surveillance.

He maintains an active security clearance with his commitment to the U.S. Government which also allows him continual access to specialized training not available to those fully entrenched in the private sector. Mr. Panico is a recipient of the

Military Intelligence Corps Association Knowlton Award and over 30 U.S. Department of Defense and U.S. Department of State service awards.

Mr. Panico holds an M.S. in Criminal Justice with a concentration in Law Enforcement and Crime Prevention from the University of Cincinnati. He also holds a B.A. in Intelligence Studies from American Military University and an A.A.S in Intelligence Operations Studies from Cochise College.

INDEX

University of
   California
   Riverside
   Evidence
   Program, 15

V

value-based fees,
   22, 101, 142,
   146–151
velocity, 38
vicarious liability,
   107, 182
Video Audio
   Timestamp
   Software (VATS),
   165, 180
Virginia, 2, 45–46,
   65, 86, 135,
   175, 197
Virtual Private
   Networks (VPN),
   169

W

Washington , 44
Washington D.C.,
   1, 44, 46, 135
Weiss, Dr. Alan, 146
WeWork, 55
Wheelwright,Tom,
   208

   Wicklander-Zulawski,
   193
Wix, 61

WordPress, 61
workers
   compensation,
   21–23, 93, 116,
   120
World Association of
   Detectives
   (WAD), 191
Wyoming, 41–42,
   45

Z

Zellow, 166,
   168–169

CPSIA information can be obtained
at www.ICGtesting.com
Printed in the USA
LVHW111123240522
719612LV00003B/50